BI-CENTENARY REUNION

OF THE

DESCENDANTS

OF

LOUIS AND JACQUES DU BOIS

(Emigrants to America, 1660 and 1675),

AT

NEW PALTZ, NEW YORK, 1875.

Honore ton Père et ta Mère.

Gedenkt der vorige Dagen.

Surely there was no such Passover kept since the days of the Fathers.

COMPILED FOR THE FAMILY CONNECTION.

THREE HUNDRED AND TWENTY-FIVE COPIES.

PHILADELPHIA:
PRESS OF RUE & JONES.
1876.

INTRODUCTORY.

Every kind of convention has been called together, in this active, associative day of ours, but none more remarkable than the one whose doings we are about to set in order. We say not this to bespeak surprise or admiration, but simply to secure attention.

What man, what brotherhood, starting out in life, can promise to themselves, two centuries after, a large assemblage of their own progeny, met to do honor to their memory? Alas, how easily we ignore the ancestor that we never saw, even no further off than a grandfather! Or, how chilling and heartless would be a meeting of a dozen or a score—all that is left of that descent!

How this convention came to be appointed, is not the least interesting of the transactions, and will form a part of these collections. But this is the place to say, and we do it with pride and pleasure (enabled to do it by the careful if not complete census of our President), that those who were present, on one or both days at New Paltz, or at the final meeting at Kingston, came from every township and village (almost) in Ulster, N. Y.;

From the counties of Dutchess, Columbia, Sullivan, Herkimer, Greene, Albany, Chemung, Oneida, Kings, Richmond or Staten Island (perhaps others in N. Y.), and the city of New York;

From Freehold, and elsewhere in Monmouth, from Somerset, and from Bridgeton, New Jersey;

From Philadelphia, Bucks and Chester counties, Pennsylvania;
From Providence, Rhode Island;
From Michigan, Illinois, Wisconsin, each one or two.

Representatives from Connecticut and Minnesota were expected, but could not be present.

Besides the *propriæ personæ*, we had letters of fellowship from shipboard, and from various parts of the land, as far as Oregon.

After weeks of wet and unpleasant weather, which made the prospect doubtful, the skies suddenly cleared before our meeting, and we were granted bright and delightful days. Without this beneficent change, our preparations would have well nigh come to nothing. "Man proposes; God disposes."

We had also a most eligible place of meeting; few country churches are so spacious. It had recently been enlarged and adorned at an expense which illustrates the ability and liberality of the congregation. The house will seat more than one thousand persons; and for most of the time was well filled. The elegant church at Kingston, in which the final meeting was held, had also a very considerable attendance, but not so great as at New Paltz.

Only a few portraits have been sent, in pursuance of the general invitation. This is matter of regret, as it leaves out many whose faces all would wish to look upon.

Of the multitude of books issuing from the press, very few are destined, or even intended, to live longer than a few years. How satisfactory it is to feel *sure* that *this* book will be in existence a century hence, and probably a great while longer. One liberal promoter of the movement has fervently said, that "every Du Bois will prize this record next to his Bible." Certainly, it should grow in interest to each succeeding generation.

We make this salutatory obeisance, simply as the Secretaries of the re-union, appointed to collect and print the proceedings; and hope the performance will prove acceptable.

Although this book is not for the public a few copies are deposited with prominent historical societies; and one with the consistory of each of the two churches where we met. It is printed by subscription, and without profit to any one.

The *pictures* are produced by the new heliotype process, and are therefore exact copies, not art-imitations.

WILLIAM E. DU BOIS.
PATTERSON DU BOIS.

ORGANIZATION.

On Wednesday morning, August 25, 1875, shortly after the ringing of the bell, the assembly was seated and called to order in the Reformed Church at New Paltz. They had previously exchanged greetings and introduction on the green sward around the edifice; and for the first time each experienced the unique pleasure of joining with many of the same name and the same remote ancestor. They all looked back to Chrétien [Christian] DuBois, of Artois, in France, who lived nearly three centuries ago, and whose two sons became Americans. Besides these, there were many, equal sharers in the blood, but of other surnames, with not a few who were only interested as spectators of a curious scene.

On the platform were seated Rev. Dr. Philip Peltz, pastor of the church; Rev. Dr. Anson DuBois, of Flatlands, Long Island; Rev. Robert P. DuBois, of New London, Chester county, Penna.; and Cornelius DuBois, Esq., of Staten Island, N. Y.

After a voluntary on the organ, the meeting was opened with prayer by the President, Dr. Anson Du Bois.

Psalm cxv., in metre, was sung by the congregation, led by the organ and choir.

The President read the letter of invitation, addressed to himself, as follows:—

New Paltz, N. Y., September 22, 1873.

Dear Brother.

The Consistory of the "Reformed Protestant Dutch Congregation of New Paltz," having understood that the descendants and kindred of Louis Du Bois, the first elder of this church, design to unite in commemorative services, hereby cordially invite them to hold such services in the church at the New Paltz, and extend the widest hospitality to all who may be pleased to attend. (Signed by the Pastor.)

The President stated that, after due deliberation, a preliminary meeting was held at the Astor House, New York, October 21, 1874, at which the following persons were present:—

GILBERT DUBOIS, of Napanoch, Ulster county, New York.
ANSON DUBOIS, Flatlands, Long Island.
ELIJAH DUBOIS, Kingston, N. Y.
PETER J. DUBOIS, Kingston, N. Y.
BENJAMIN DUBOIS, Freehold, N. J.
T. VANDERVEER DUBOIS, Freehold, N. J.
DR. HENRY A. DUBOIS, New Haven, Conn.
JAMES G. DUBOIS, New York.
EUGENE DUBOIS, New York.
PATTERSON DUBOIS, Philadelphia.

At that session, of three hours, the matter was fairly inaugurated; and at a meeting of the executive committee, May 17, 1875 (also in New York city), the arrangements were, as far as possible, completed. Rev. Dr. Anson Du Bois was (at the first meeting) unanimously chosen to preside, and Patterson Du Bois to act as Secretary.

Notices were issued in various papers and in circular letters, with a view to reach all branches of the connection.

The Pastor of the church then addressed the following welcome to the assembly:—

It is my privilege, in behalf of this ancient church, to welcome the descendants and kindred of Louis Du Bois to this house, and to our homes. As the eyes of the church are turned back to events which transpired two centuries ago, your honored ancestor occupies a very large place in the picture before us. Without trenching in the slightest degree upon the province of the historian whose labors are to afford us instruction and delight, I take up the very first page of our record as a church, and there we find the honorable prominence of Louis Du Bois. The record is as follows. It has received a slight editing, which shows the changes of two hundred years in the French language. And I may remark, it is evidently his hand-writing:—

Le 22 de Janv [Janvier] 1683 monsier pierre daillie ministre de la parole de dieu est arive [arrivé] au nouveau palatinat et presca [precha] deux fois le dimance [Dimanche] suivant et proposa au ceef [chefs] des famille de coisir [choisir] a plus de vois [voix] par les peres de famille un ancien et un diake [diacre] ce qu il firt [qu'ils firent] et coisirt [choisirent] Louys du bois pour ancien et hughe frere pour diake pour ayder le ministre a conduire les membres de leglise [l'eglise] quil sasemble [qui s'assemble] au nouveau palatinat lequel furt confirme [lesquels furent confirmés] ensuite dans ladict carge [charge] dancien et diake. Le present liuur [livre] a est faict [a été fait] pour mestre [mettre] les choses quil apatien [qui appartiennent] a la dict eglise.

The following is a translation:—

"The 22d of January, 1683, Mr. Pierre Daillie, minister of the Word of God, arrived at New Paltz, and preached twice on the following Sunday, and proposed to the heads of the families that they should choose by majority of votes, by the fathers of families, one elder and one deacon, which they did, and chose Louis DuBois for elder and Hugh Frère for deacon, to assist the minister in guiding the members of the church that meets in New Paltz; who were subsequently confirmed in the said charge of elder and deacon. This minute has been made to put in order the matters which pertain to the said church."

Without interfering with your arrangements in connection with this celebration, the church in New Paltz, called by your fathers "*l'eglise de Nouveau Palatinat*," feels that her history is too closely connected with the name and fame of your ancestor to suffer her to have no part in according fit honors to the first elder of the church.

Accordingly, you have been invited to hold your meetings in this house, and otherwise partake of our hospitality. Though as a church we have no influence or control over your exercises here, we assure you that we expect to enjoy them in scarcely less measure than any of you, who may be "Du Boises on both sides," and all the way down from the patriarch Louis.

This church, of which Louis DuBois was the first elder, was established in 1683—a French Reformed Church, as strictly Huguenot as any association of protestant Christians in France. For fifty years the language of our record is French, succeeded by the Low Dutch for seventy years more. Since the beginning of the present century, the English has been our church vernacular.

In 1720, the DuBoises and their cotemporaries, having built a house of worship, prepared and recorded the deed of settlement, which gave each family its appointed share of seats in the church. Only their pious spirit could have accomplished this work, where there were only twenty-one heads of families. The expression of thanks and praise to God, for having put it in their hearts to build a house for the Lord, lives in the following antiquated French record:—

Beni sois Dieu Quij L nous a mys a coeur de Luy batir une maison pour y estre adores et servir et que par sa grace nous Lavon finys eu Lan Dix vii et Dieu veillie que son evangile y soit anonce dean ce ciecle et dedan Lautre y usque au jour De Leternite. Amen.

They needed a French teacher; but it is easily translated:—

Blessed be God, who has put it into our hearts to build a house where He may be adored and served, and that by his grace we have finished it in the year 17 [1717]; and God grant that his gospel may be preached here from one age to another till the day of eternity. Amen.

Most heartily do I congratulate you upon so honorable and reverend an ancestry. The Huguenots are beginning to be reckoned at something of their proper worth. Foremost in prosperity and weight of character, among the Huguenot settlements of America, is this of *Nouveau Palatinat.* This singular, and to us residents, very agreeable result is doubtless owing to the wise fraternity governed so long by their own "twelve men," representing the Huguenot tribes. These leaders of the Paltz Israel have continued in succession down to the time of those now living. One gentleman sits before me to-day who has been chosen the representative of his tribe. This wise, active legislation—for it was legislative action—must have been greatly moulded by Louis Du Bois, the acknowledged leader of the Huguenot colony which settled upon the ground we occupy.

Some of you whose clans have gone out from the parent house in the past generation, have achieved higher fame in the world, and surpassed your cousins, who cultivate the ancestral acres, in putting money in the purse. But all feel that the highest earthly virtue is that reverence for ancestry which the old Romans knew by the honorable name of *piety.* In that virtue you all have great inducements to share, for Louis Du Bois and his colleagues builded wisely, when they laid the foundation, and set up, or stood up themselves, the pillars of this community.

You will entirely agree with me when I say, that the relations of your ancestors to the church crown his memory with special honor, and deserve, as they receive, your deepest veneration for his official ecclesiastical life. No wonder that his descendants should desire to have this relationship inscribed on the stones which tell where their dust sleeps. Just here you and this church are brought into close sympathy. Our humble share with you in this celebration arises from locality. So we open to you our plain Huguenot homes, and invite you into our place of worship, the third successor of that built by the Huguenot fathers.

Trusting that your visit among us will be an unalloyed pleasure, and hopeful of very interesting and valuable results in regard to many points of history which you will elucidate, we give you welcome, which if plain, is most cordial. You are to be congratulated in having such an ancestry. There is no need of your seeking refuge from ancient family dishonor in the genealogy which "development" provides. On the other hand, my preaching habit in this place so far overcomes me, that I beg you to feel that your relations to our honored elder gives a *prestige* to you and your children, which you should count among the most valuable of your inherited possessions, as you seek to be faithful to your advantages.

Congratulating you upon your reunion, and the ample arrangements of your executive committee for pleasantly and advantageously passing your time in connection with this visit, I put the feelings of the church and community in one hearty word, as I again bid you WELCOME.*

Psalm cv. was read, and prayer offered by Rev. Robert P. Du Bois.

Hymn 624 was sung, by choir and congregation.

The President addressed the meeting:—

We are met, dear brethren, that we may suitably commemorate the mercies of the Lord to our fathers and their children

* This graceful welcome was the more *bienvenu*, as the speaker had no consanguinity with us, save as we are "all of one blood." (EDS.)

during the past two hundred years. You have imposed the great task of giving expression to our gratitude upon one unworthy of the honor, and inadequate to the duty. Only in the honesty and earnestness of my endeavor, and in the devoutness of my spirit, which seeks the true baptism of the hour, am I the fit interpreter of your emotions, or the officiating minister in your worship.

While I speak in behalf of our family, I cannot for a moment be unconscious that I am among those whose hearts thrill in perfect unison with our own; many of them, though bearing other names, inherit as fully as ourselves the blood of our ancestors, and whose joy at this moment is as exuberant as our own. Our words of thanksgiving, therefore, are also theirs.

First of all we bless God for bringing our fathers to this place. They came out of great tribulation, but the angel of his presence kept them. With hope in their hearts, and calm resolve in their countenances, had they pressed through all obstacles, until here He gave them the heritage of the heathen.

Fly back on fancy's wing, and kindle up your gratitude among them. They have emerged from the forest. The sun is in the west. His rays give the clear outline of these mountains, and cast the soft and deepening shadows along the further verge of the valley. The gentle waters beside them flow in refreshing sweetness. The earth, the sky, the waters, even the birds are still. But God is in the earth and sky and water; God is in the evening shadows and in the silence.

A green spot beside the stream receives them. You see them in the dim distance of the years, but there is a divine eye watching each one in faithful love.

Is their journey ended? Yes, their flight from their own dear France—like timid hares, with the whole pack let loose after them; their wanderings in strange countries, their perils on the sea, their exposures in a new world among those differing in ancestry, habits and language—yes, here their journey ends; weary, woeful, through the valley of death had they come. But the long night of sorrow ends now, and joy cometh in the morning!

Thanks be unto God for the victory! Theirs it is—a great achievement of faith and patience, and true nobility of soul: a glory to those who won it, and to our God, who prompted and guided, and made successful all their endeavors.

Tradition tells us that that exiled band gathered close together on the first evening of their arrival here. They gathered for worship. Thank God; many times have they done so since that day. Then nature was their temple, with sky for roof, mountains for columns, and the earth itself for altar, and through all the great presence of God!

They opened their father's Bible,—their hearts waited for the word. With reverence they kneeled, or stood, with bowed heads, or sat upon the grass, the mother with the children. And the word fell softly as the dews. The word fell soothingly as the sunset. It was the twenty-third Psalm they read—beginning with "The Lord is my Shepherd; I shall not want," &c.

Oh! words most precious to heavy souls! Words full of rest after toil, of safety after danger, of joy after grief, of hope, nay, assurance after fear, doubts and agonies of suspense!

And then the song arose, the harmony of many voices, with sweeter, half-hidden note of sister, wife and child. And with the hush of the song arose the voice of prayer full of holy joy, deep thankfulness, and heartfelt, reassuring repose in God.

Thus our fathers worshipped at the "Tri-Cor." Thus that feeble, exiled company, strong only in God and in one another, entered upon their earthly inheritance. Their martyred brethren had then already entered into glory, and they themselves have now long ago joined the throng of God's redeemed saints. But their song shall never die. We their children will react their faith in God. We will repeat their worship. We will revive again their grateful joy, and roll it onward with undiminished unction and power to those who are to come after us.

After two hundred years, we come to these hallowed scenes to bless the God of our fathers, and to bear witness to all His faithfulness and love. Here, where a pious ancestry, who, for freedom of conscience and the love of the truth, had forsaken homes and estates, and titles, and kindred, and country, and braved the dangers of sea and land, gave themselves in humility and sincerity to the Lord, we, their children, come in a devout pilgrimage to set up once more their banners, and inscribe upon them anew,

Jehovah Shalom—"*The Lord send peace.*" Here, and to-day, do we bless God for preserving our fathers' heritage, both temporal and spiritual, in this place, and in extending like mercies among all the dispersed descendants. Witnesses are we of the divine mercies—of the divine faithfulness; and His name alone do we exalt in thanksgiving and praise. For all these years our banner —*The Lord send peace*—has waved from this church founded by our fathers. Peace has flowed as constant as the full river at our side. Uninterrupted prosperity has here gathered her annual harvests. Here have we enjoyed homes of comfort, the facilities of education, the respect of men, and the institutions of the religion of Jesus Christ, the most valued and fruitful of all these blessings. And to-day the old Bible faith is preached, and sung, and believed, and loved in its holy simplicity, its purifying power in heart and character, its divine and blessed unction of immortal life as our fathers loved it, and lived and died upon it. And here in the church of our fathers have been, and are to-day, no crude theories of religion, no dalliance with Rome's irrecoverable apostacy from saving truth to satanic and worldly craft, no compromise with science, "falsely so called."

In the gospel of Jesus Christ, our fathers found these words: "Verily, I say unto you, there is no man that hath left home or parents, or brethren or wife, or children for the kingdom of God's sake, who shall not receive manifold more in this present time, and in the world to come everlasting life." My brethren, this promise is indeed fulfilled in us as it now is, yet more gloriously in our fathers. It was the religion of Jesus Christ that made our fathers what they were, brought us where we are, and gave us what we have. Let us heartily exclaim, "Not unto us, O Lord, not unto us, but unto thy name give glory for thy mercy and thy Truth's sake."

At the conclusion of this Address, the President read the following HYMN OF THANKSGIVING, written for the occasion, without giving the author's name.

To thank our God, our fathers' God,
With joy your hearts and voices raise;
And we will all in songs unite
With you, to celebrate His praise.

They jeered our fathers; Romish priests
Did call them Huguenots in scorn.
"We 'll burn the heretics," they said,
"The beggars vile, the 'Gueux' forlorn."

They brought the fagot, fired the pile;
They thought the Papal bull would do;
They burnt the heretics, and tried
Inquisitorial tortures too.

Nor sword, nor fire, nor mortal pain
Could their undaunted courage move:
The word of God sustained them then;
Such cruel deaths their faith did prove.

"Bow down, and worship me, ye slaves!
And save your lives, your goods and lands,
For I am Christ's vicegerent here,
And lay on you his just commands."

"Oh! Pope of Rome," our fathers said,
"To Christ alone we 'll bow the knee;
From service such as yours, our Lord
And only God hath set us free.

"Let earthly kings and worldly men
Acknowledge thee a god on earth;
Thy ghostly might o'er them extend,
But we have rights of heavenly birth.

"A right to read God's holy word,
To guide our conscience by the light
It sheds upon the path of all
Who would the flesh and devil fight.

"And we are told, and know it true,
There is a land beyond the sea;
And God hath bid us seek a home
Where we may worship and be free.

"Farewell to France! Our native land
And all we have we leave behind—
Our arms are strong, our hearts are brave;
There peace and plenty we will find."

And to this land our fathers came,
'T is now two hundred years ago,
And God hath blessed them and their sons
With all that 's needful here below.

And here we meet to praise His name
For all His mercies and His grace,
And for the honor He vouchsafed
To Louis, James, and all our race.

Then thank our God, our fathers' God,
With joy your hearts and voices raise—
And we will all in hymns unite
With you to celebrate His praise.

Mr. Cornelius Du Bois then read the following paper, on

OUR HISTORY IN EUROPE.

Friends and Fellow Kinsmen.

The occasion which has called us together this day, should fill us not only with love and gratitude to God, our Heavenly Father, but also with good-will and kind feelings towards each other.

I must claim your indulgence, and bespeak your favorable regards for the paper which I have been requested to prepare and present to you, on the history of our family and its connections in France, down to the leaving of Louis Du Bois for America.

This task was originally assigned to a near relative of mine, who, by reason of ill-health and remote residence, has been unable to undertake it, or even to be present with us at this time. His knowledge of the subject, and his professional pursuits, would have enabled him to lay before you a far more interesting discourse than it is in my power to do.*

Having, however, a strong desire, in common with you all, to do honor to the memory of Louis Du Bois, who, I believe, was the first protestant of the name who came to this country, which at that time was called, as it was in fact, the *New World*—I have not felt at liberty to decline your committee's invitation to be my brother's substitute, and to address you with such facts and considerations relating to the history of our ancestors, and to the time in which they lived, before their emigration to this country, as I might, with my limited knowledge of the subject, be able to gather and set before you.

I say "*our* ancestors;" for though not a lineal descendant of your progenitor Louis, yet there can be no doubt, I think, that Jacques Du Bois, from whom I am descended, was not only a contemporary and associate, but also a very near relative of his.

They were both born in the same neighborhood, near LaBassée, in the province of Artois, in France. The kingdom has since

* The reference was to Rev. Geo. W. Du Bois, of Faribault, Minnesota. We are greatly indebted to the scholarship and patient research of this gentleman, and his brothers. The *Jacques Chart* will be cited hereafter. (Eds.)

been divided into departments, and Artois is known at the present day as the "Department of Pas du-Calais."

Each sought an asylum in the New World, where he could worship God after the dictates of his own conscience. Louis at first went to Manheim, in the Palatinate; and Jacques (or James, as it is in English) went to Leyden, in Holland. Afterwards their home on this continent was in the same locality in Ulster county, New York; and there they were again united by the strong bonds of Christian fellowship and, as is quite probable, of *brotherly* affection.

Louis was married at Manheim, in October, 1655, and Jacques at Leyden, in April, 1663. The marriage record of Jacques, at Leyden, says that he was from the vicinity of LaBassée, which was in the province of Artois.

Jacques, however, did not arrive at Esopus till some fifteen years after Louis was settled there. The letters of church-membership, or letters of dismissal from the church of the Walloons, at Leyden, which he took with him on leaving that city, are dated 15th April, 1675, as is evidenced by the church records still extant. He must have died at Esopus, the same or the succeeding year, as in the old records of Ulster county there is still preserved a document by which it appears that his widow, Pieronne Bentÿn, was married again to a John Pietersy, who, as such husband, and for a small consideration to himself personally, in December, 1677, contracts with Matthew Blanshan (who was the father-in-law of Louis Du Bois) to pledge to him the lands belonging to Jacques Du Bois, in Ryssel, Flanders, as also the rents which the said lands had earned, for the fulfilment of the conditions of a contract which said Jacques Du Bois, in his lifetime, had made with said Blanshan. The nature or object of the contract does not in this document appear, but as Pieronne Bentÿn is described in her marriage record with Jacques Du Bois, at Leyden, as of Lisle (which is the same as Ryssel in Flanders), it may be that the lands referred to were held partly or altogether in right of the wife. Else there would seem to be no good reason why Pietersy should be called upon to confirm Du Bois's contract with Blanshan.

On leaving Leyden, in 1675, Jacques had put on record a procuration or power of attorney to sell his house in that city. He is described in the Leyden records as a manufacturer of gros-grains, coarse-grained fabrics of silk, cloth, etc.

His three sons were at the time of his death of tender age—the eldest, Jacques (afterwards known by the translation of the name into Dutch as Jacobus), was born at Leyden, and baptized by the name of Jacques, in March, 1665. John, in July, 1671, and Pierre (known here as Pieter), my ancestor, and the ancestor of the Dutchess county branch of the family, was born at Leyden, March 17th, 1674, and was therefore only about three years of age when his mother, it seems, was married to Pietersy, at Kingston.

In his name, and on behalf of his descendants who are invited to this reunion of the Du Bois family—invited as the descendants of a kinsman of Louis Du Bois—I here wish, All hail! to you, his posterity; and we gladly unite with you in these commemorative services in honor of the founder and the first elder of this church at New Paltz, feeling deeply sensible of the great obligation and debt of gratitude we owe to his memory for those benign and Christian influences which his life and character exerted over all about him, and under the operation of which Pierre Du Bois was nurtured in childhood, and grew up to manhood, a sincere, active and eminently pious Christian.

I state it on the authority of my honored friend, your kinsman, Gilbert Du Bois, Esq., of Napanoch, that his name is prominent both as deacon and elder in the church records of Kingston, Poughkeepsie and Fishkill.

And as further evidence that there must have been a near relationship between our respective ancestors, I might add, that Peter grew up at Kingston, and there married, October 12th, 1697, Jannetje Burhans, daughter of Jan Burhans, of Brabant, and that he perpetuated the name of Chrétien Du Bois, who was the father of your Louis Du Bois, by naming his third son *Christian*, who also named his only son *Christian.* They were grandfather and great-grandfather to my esteemed relative, Doctor Abram Du Bois, a prominent physician of the city of New York.

Both Louis and Jacques Du Bois were Walloons.

Louis in this country was called, *par excellence*, *The Walloon.*

Jacques baptized all his children in the protestant church, called the Church of the Walloons, at Leyden.

The language they spoke was the old French dialect of Picardy, or langue d'Oui, as it was called, which preserved, more than the langue d'Oc of the southern province, the remnants of the old Gallic tongue; and into it were incorporated from time to time, from their contact and intercourse with other people, words of German and Norman origin. From the three dialects of Picardy, Normandy and Burgundy has been derived the pure French of the present day.

The records of this church at New Paltz furnish specimens of the language as then in use in the handwriting of Louis Du Bois, its first elder, which appear very antique and odd, but which are perfectly intelligible to a French scholar.

The Walloons were by nature and descent a brave and hardy race, and when the provinces, known as the Walloon provinces had passed under the dominion of Spain, the king selected his household troops, known as the "Walloon Guards," from that intrepid people.

At the time of the Roman conquest, Artois was a part of Belgic Gaul, and Cæsar himself, in the first lines of his history of the Gallic war, bears indisputable evidence to the valor and prowess of the inhabitants of that part of the country.

Every tyro in Latin is familiar with the opening of Cæsar's Commentaries. And our esteemed kinsmen from Philadelphia, now present with us, must bear with me for reminding them of their school-boy days. How carefully their revered father, the Rev. Uriah Du Bois, drilled them and all his pupils in the rudiments of the Latin tongue; and when sufficiently advanced to take up Cæsar, with what self-satisfaction they began to translate "Gallia est omnis divisa in partes tres:" "All Gaul is divided into three parts."

Judging from the simplicity of the opening sentences, there was no difficulty in mastering this great author. They never imagined they would come to Cæsar's bridge, which they would find so difficult to get over. And when in the succeeding lines he designates the inhabitants of these three parts as the Belgæ, the Aquitani, and the Celtæ, and says, "Horum omnium fortissimi sunt Belgæ,"—"Of all these, the bravest are the Belgæ,"—how little did they suspect that the mighty conqueror, the greatest warrior of antiquity, was paying a tribute of respect to the courage, the hardihood, and warlike character of their own remote forefathers!

These warlike Belgæ inhabited the northeasterly part of Gaul, on the borders of the English channel and the northern or German ocean; while the Celtæ inhabited the middle portion, running from northwest to southeast; and the Aquitani dwelling in the southwest part, bordered on the ocean, now called the Bay of Biscay.

Belgic Gaul, in which that province of France afterwards known as Artois was located, had been conquered by the Romans about fifty years before the Christian era. It remained under the power and domination of the Roman empire until the invasion of the Franks, a neighboring German tribe, in 418. They, under their king, Clovis (the founder of the Merovingian dynasty), conquered the greater part of ancient Gaul, in 486, and gave to it the name of France. This dynasty, or first race of kings, continued till 752, when Pepin le Bref (or the Short), son of Charles Martel (or the Hammer), and father of Charlemagne, seized upon the throne; and from him sprang the second race of rulers, known as the Carlovingian dynasty, which lasted two hundred and thirty-five years. On the death of Louis V., the last of those kings, in 987, Hugh Capet, Duke of Orleans and Count of Paris, usurped the crown, and was the first of that enduring race of kings, or third race, of which the Valois, the Orleans, and the Bourbons were offshoots, and which is known in history as the Capetian dynasty. With this able monarch began the policy of reannexing to the crown those extensive domains and provinces into which the kingdom was divided, and which at his accession were governed and held in sovereign right by feudal lords, who, like himself, had become more powerful than the king to whom they owed allegiance.

It has not been without a certain design that I have thus presented to you a sketch of the history of the land of our forefathers, from the invasion of Julius Cæsar to the establishment upon the throne of France of the kings of the Capetian dynasty, about the close of the tenth century; for a proper elucidation of my subject makes it necessary that I should, in a cursory manner, call your attention to the feudal system, which at this time was the basis of all government throughout the kingdom and its provinces.

With the Merovingian conquerors it had been introduced into France, and under the Carlovingians it had taken firm root and had pervaded the whole kingdom, so that all the land was held by feudal tenure, and the laboring classes—cultivators of the soil —constituting the greatest part of the inhabitants of the country, were reduced to a state of abject servitude.

They were either literally *slaves*—the absolute property of their masters, having no personal rights whatever—or they were *villains*, who were not, strictly speaking, slaves; for after paying the owner a fixed rent, they were nominally entitled to the products of the land they cultivated: still they belonged to the soil, and were transferable with it; or else they were *freemen*, so called, many of whom, from the severe exactions imposed upon them, preferred, and actually entered into, the state of bondage. These owned a part of the land they cultivated; but in consideration thereof, they were obliged to cultivate another portion for the benefit of the real owner.

It was a fundamental principle, "Nulle terre sans Seigneur," or, as we would say in English, "No lord, no land," and every landholder was bound to appear in arms for the defence of his superior.

It was in the eleventh century also that *surnames* were first assumed as a distinctive mark of nobility, and if a French surname can be traced back to the eleventh century, it is indisputable evidence that the family entitled to it was, at that time, a noble one. Our surname, Du Bois, was of feudal origin, and was at least as early as this (1066) century, as will presently appear.

The *roturiers*, or common people, were not allowed a surname, which in after times they received from their occupations, peculiar circumstances characterizing the person, or causes existing other than those which designate the possession of office, or the holding of lands.

This feudal system, with its titles and designations of nobility, was not known in England till after its conquest by William of Normandy. The Anglo-Saxons, always jealous of their freedom and individual rights, adopted the laws and government imposed upon them by the conqueror, with modifications of their own; but at that time they first became acquainted with the system of feudal rights and usages which William I. brought from Normandy, and from that time they date their aristocracy.

The surname of "du Bois" was an ancient family name, both in Artois and Normandy, before William I., King of England, left his native shores, and it has remained unchanged to the present day.

This brings me to the first historic mention of the name of "du Bois" in France.

In the heraldic records preserved in the royal library of Paris, under the head of "du Bois," it is expressly said that the family of that name is one of the oldest of the noble families of the bailiwick of Cotentin, in Normandy. It begins the genealogy with Geoffroi du Bois, describing him as a knight banneret under William the Conqueror, whom he accompanied to the conquest of England, in 1066.

And it is carried on in seventeen regular descents in the eldest male line, all of whom are designated as Seigneurs and Chevaliers, till it ends with Louisa Du Bois, wife of Charles Du Bois, Seigneur of l'Espinay and of Pirou, who married his cousin in the fourth degree, and by whom he had two daughters—the one Claude, Lady of l'Espinay le Tesson and of Pirou, the wife of the Marquis of Bressey (she died in 1648), and the other daughter, Mary, married Philippe de Bouillé, Count of Créancé.

The genealogy then goes back to about the year 1448, and takes up the line of descent from the second son of Thomas Du-Bois, Seigneur of Pirou and of l'Espinay, who was the twelfth in succession of the line of eldest sons from Geoffroi, first mentioned.

This second son of Thomas was also named Geoffroi, and of his posterity the fourth in descent was Charles, who had thus united the two branches by his marriage with Louisa.

The Seignory of Pirou had been acquired by the marriage of Thomas' father, John Du Bois, called of Gascoigne, Seigneur of l'Espinay le Tesson, with Catherine de la Luzerne, Dame de

Pirou. And the Seignory of l'Espinay le Tesson had been previously acquired by the marriage of Thomas' great-grandfather, Monseigneur Jean Du Bois, knight banneret, with Françoise de Tesson, Dame de l'Espinay le Tesson.

This united line, terminating in daughters, as we have before mentioned, the genealogy then goes back to a younger brother of Thomas, who was named Raoul Du Bois, for the third line or branch.

Raoul's son, Richard Du Bois, chevalier, was the father of Robert Du Bois, who, the record says, made proof of his nobility in 1540. Why this was necessary does not appear. Two causes may be assigned. He may have been a protestant and recanted his faith, for Francis I., the persecutor of the Calvinists, was then upon the throne; or it may have been that having, as a younger son of a younger branch, become a commoner, he had to make proof of his descent from a noble family to entitle himself to court privileges.

There is no mention made of his children. Nothing is said of his having no issue; and no cause is assigned, as in other cases, for discontinuing the record in his line. If his posterity adhered to the new religion, it sufficiently accounts for a discontinuance of the record.

This genealogical record speaks of a Du Bois, Seigneur de l'Etang Belhôtel, in Normandy, of the district of Alençon, as a family maintained in its nobility, the 8th May, 1667. The persecutor, Louis XIV., was then King of France, and, to their shame be it said, many nobles who had before adhered to the reformed religion were, in his reign, induced by motives of policy to abjure their faith.

In this year (1667), your progenitor, Louis Du Bois, was already seven years in America.

The record also says that François, and his son Charles Du Bois, Seigneurs of Belhôtel, had sold, prior to the year 1654, the Seignory of La Trenaye Fayel to William d'Ormont, Seigneur d'Aubry le Panthon. This was six years after the peace of Westphalia, of which I shall have occasion to speak hereafter, and is a transaction compatible with protestantism.

Under the head of Du Bois de Givri and Du Bois de Leuville,

mention is at first made of John Du Bois, Seigneur de Fontaines, maitre d'hôtel (or steward of the household) of Charles VIII. He died in 1507.

His son John married, 17th October, 1493, the niece of the chancellor of France. He was king's councillor and comptroller-general of the finances. He had several sons, one of whom was Astremoine Du Bois. In 1569, the king gave him a *safe conduct* on account of his services and those of his predecessors.

The king, be it remembered, was the miserable Charles IX., under whose sanction, and the contrivance of the intriguing and ambitious queen-mother, Catherine de Medici, the massacre of St. Bartholomew took place, in 1572. It is believed that about one hundred thousand of the reformed religion (Sully says sixty thousand) were massacred at that time in France.

Astremoine, at the time he received his safe conduct, was evidently a protestant, and it would seem that he afterwards, for political reasons, renounced his faith, as did the chivalrous Henry of Navarre, the great friend of the protestant cause, who saved his life in the St. Bartholomew massacre, as did also the Prince of Condé, by recantation before the king. Henry afterwards took the field at the head of thirty thousand Huguenots, but to secure himself upon the throne, as Henry IV. of France, he again changed his religion, and gave in his adhesion to the Roman church.

In 1584, Astremoine Du Bois, under Henry III., was restored to his nobility, and was declared to be descended by ancientry, or dignity of birth, from "la maison Du Bois en *Artois*," the Du Bois family of *Artois*.

He had three sons, Antoine, Charles and Astremoine. His eldest son, Antoine, was the Seigneur de Fontaines, and married in 1571. He was king's councillor, and ambassador in the Pays Bas, or Netherlands.

Of his children, the record goes on to state, we only know or recognize Pierre Du Bois, who served in the army in 1597.—(Henry IV. was then a catholic king.)

This Pierre Du Bois, Seigneur of Fontaines Morau, married Françoise Olivier de Leuville, by whom he had several children. The eldest was John, of whom nothing more is said.

Another son was Louis Du Bois, designated as Seigneur de Fontaines Morau et DuPlessis, grand bailli de Tourraine, lieutenant-general of the armies of the king. By letters of the month of December, 1653 (under Louis XIV.), recorded in parliament, (the high courts of judicature were called parliaments in France, and any act, to become a law, had to be first registered in parliament,) the Seignory of Givri, acquired by his marriage, was raised to a Marquisate. He died the 13th December, 1699, at the age of eighty-three years. He had taken for his second wife Françoise Morau, Dame de la Garonne, and their posterity became extinct in 1684. This was twenty-four years after Louis had left for this country. The next year (1685) was the revocation of the edict of Nantes, by Louis XIV. It had been given by his grandfather, Henry IV., in April, 1598, and so had been nominally in force eighty-seven years.

The Marquisate de Leuville was inherited by Louis Du Bois de Fiennes, the Marquis of Givri, and from him the genealogy is continued down to the Marchioness of Poyanne, who died at Paris, in 1761, aged thirty-three years.

This noble family, being descended from Astremoine, trace back their lineage to the house of Du Bois *in Artois*. And it is from this original stock that all collateral branches deduce their origin.

When William of Normandy had achieved the conquest of England, it is quite probable that Geoffroi Du Bois, who had joined his banner, as we have seen, on his return to France, received for his services the bailiwick of Cotentin in the dukedom of Normandy. But it matters not whether the original seat of the family was Artois or Normandy. The surname proves that all who bear it were of the same origin. In feudal times it could not belong to two families without the addition of an agnomen, and there are now in France and Belgium many such added names attached to the surname of Du Bois, to distinguish separate branches having a common origin.

A German historian remarks, that no family names occur in German history before the middle of the eleventh century. The oldest trace of them, he says, is in 1062, when a Henricus *de Sinna* is mentioned in Schannat's Buchonia Veteri. In France, they were somewhat earlier.

But neither lands nor offices were at first hereditary. They became inheritable on the continent about the beginning of the eleventh century, and were not so in England until after the conquest. In monarchial governments at that time, as in the present day in all kingdoms of Europe, except in Norway (where, by the constitution of 1814, "no hereditary privileges, personal or real, can be conferred on any native of Norway"), the inheritance of lands and titles passed to the eldest son. And in France, until the revolution, the younger sons had either to join the army or the church, or they forfeited all claims to the consideration of the privileged classes. Any connection with mercantile business, or meaner occupation, deprived them of their ancestral prerogative of nobility. Hence all the collateral branches of a noble family very soon became reduced to the rank of the common people; but as chevaliers or priests they could maintain their birth privileges, or by marriage with a noble lady possessed of lands to which office and dignity were annexed, they became in her right feudal lords; and thus marriages were less an affair of the heart, on the bridegroom's part, than a matter of policy In this manner many of the descendants of this ancient family of Du Bois maintained not only the bare surname but their nobility also, through their intermarriages. The great majority of them, however, from the natural results of the monarchical principle I have mentioned (independently of the fiery persecutions to which our immediate forefathers were subjected for conscience sake), had nothing left them indicative of noble ancestry but the name they bore, and with it the satisfaction of a residence in their native land and the enjoyment of the property which, by talent or industry, they might acquire.

But *these* privileges of a freeman, the inalienable rights of life, liberty and property, were not conceded to our Huguenot forefathers by the bigoted despots then ruling in France and the Austrian Netherlands. They could and did most cruelly and unwisely drive them, by bloody persecutions, from their native land; they could confiscate their property and reduce them to the utmost necessities in regard to the means of livelihood; they could take their lives by fire and sword and the tortures of the inquisition, but they could not rob them of their Christian faith, nor of their old, time-honored family name.

Some of these persecuted noble families, it is true, in going to other countries and incorporating themselves with other nationalities, voluntarily renounced their ancestral names and translated them into the language of their adopted country. Thus, LeBlanc became DeWitt, LeGrand became de Groot, Du Bois became Van der Bosch.

Albert Du Bois, a cousin of my ancestor Jacques, born at Wicres, the birthplace of your ancestor Louis, records his name in the French church of the Walloons, at Leyden, as Du Bois, but afterwards, on joining the Dutch church, where other children of his were baptized, he enters it as Van der Bosch. He preserves the capital B, even in the translation of the name into the Dutch language.

In these genealogical records at Paris, from which I have given extracts, there are many other families of the name mentioned. They are all designated as barons, chevaliers, etc., and they no doubt sprang from the same stock in *Artois* or *Normandy*.

But I will only mention one more. "The family of Du Bois de Hoves, in Flanders, and in the country of Artois." That is the title.

After remarking that this family is spoken of in the history of Cambrai and of Cambressis, it begins with John Du Bois, called de Hoves, after the name of an estate which is in the Comté de Namur.

He was equery of Charles V., baillie of Dole, and married Marie de Thiennes de Hoves. (Here is an illustration of the manner in which additional names were annexed to the original surname of Du Bois, as I have before mentioned.)

His son, Zegres, was councillor and assessor to the government of Lille. He married Marie d'Herignies, and had three sons—John, who died in 1611, Baudouin and Melchior.

His son, Baudouin Du Bois, Seigneur d'Herignies, was mayor of the city of Lille. He married Barbe de Caudelle. They had three sons—Charles, Maximilian and Baudouin, and four daughters.

His son, Maximilian Du Bois, called de Hoves, Seigneur d'Herignies, was married in 1642, and had three daughters and a son—Valerand François Joseph Du Bois, called de Hoves, Seigneur d'Herignies, was married in 1672, and had two daughters and two sons. His genealogy is carried down in the line of the eldest son to 1720.

The second branch of this family is then taken up, going back to Melchior Du Bois, the second son of Zegres. His son, André Du Bois, Sieur d'Haucourt, died 11th March, 1635, leaving by his wife, Rose de Vermeil, his son, Antoine Du Bois de Hoves, Seigneur of the Barony of Fosseux.

He was councillor of the king in his provincial council of *Artois*. He died in 1688, over eighty years of age, and left seven sons and one daughter. (See the Armorial of France, Register 5.)

As the king here referred to is Louis XIV., I will state that Artois, in which province our ancestors Louis and Jacques were born, had been ceded to the king of France by Philip IV. of Spain, at the conclusion of the war between the two countries, terminated by the peace of the Pyrenees, in 1659, a peace consummated by the marriage of Louis XIV. to Maria Theresa, the Infanta of Spain.

A brief reference to the history of Artois, as it appertains to our subject, may not be uninteresting to you.

In the fifteenth century that province of France was under the Burgundian dominion. But the marriage of Maximilian I., Emperor of Germany, at that time Archduke of Austria, to Mary, the daughter and heiress of Charles the Bold, Duke of Burgundy, in 1477, had annexed the Burgundian domains and the Netherlands to the archduke's inherited estates of Austria.

Louis XI., then king of France, of the house of Valois, wrested Flanders, Artois and the duchy of Burgundy from him, and Artois for a time was again a part of France.

Louis' son, however, Charles VIII., ceded back Artois to Maximilian, on whose death, in 1519, it passed to his grandson, the Emperor Charles V., who was also Charles I. of Spain, and from him it passed to his son, the bigotted Philip II. of Spain, the husband for a time of Mary Queen of England. Tennyson, in his recently published drama of Queen Mary, describes the infatuation of the queen for this heartless monarch. They were both cruel persecutors, in their respective realms, of those professing the reformed religion. Artois had thus been for more than one hundred years under Spanish and Austrian dominion, when, by the peace of the Pyrenees, it was permanently annexed to the crown of France, in 1659.

The father of Louis Du Bois, as before remarked, was Chrétien Du Bois. He is designated in the record of his son's marriage, at Manheim, October 10th, 1655, as the deceased Chrétien Du Bois, resident of Wicres.

The records of this latter place have been examined, and I regret to say that, from age and bad ink and mutilation, the register is almost illegible.

The baptismal record shows that Chrétien Du Bois had three children baptized at Wicres. The dates made out are the 18th June, 1622, the 13th November, 1625, and the 21st October, 1626. The names are illegible, and seem to have been intentionally obliterated. These researches were made by archivists under the direction of the consul for the United States at Lille, Mons. C. Du Bois Grégoire. In his letter of 15th July, 1875, he writes that he had visited the canton of La Bassée several times, where there are very old records, but could make nothing out, as, where the Christian names occurred, the paper was torn or cut out. He further states that the registers in the village of Wicres were also in many places illegible from age, bad ink, and from being torn and worm-eaten. He says Wicres has a population of three hundred inhabitants, and that many farmers in the vicinity had pointed out to him the farm which the tradition of the country recognizes to have belonged to the Du Bois.

In a subsequent letter of the 2d August (this month), he writes (I translate his language): "It is extremely vexatious that the poor old register of Wicres should be in such a sad condition, and that the paper should be torn at the spot of the Christian names of the eldest sons of Chrétien." From the names of the sponsors, he thinks that Jacques and Louis were the "fils ainés," the two oldest sons of Chrétien. He adds: "My inmost conviction is that they are brothers, and sons of Chrétien." The copy he sends of the extract from the registers of the Etat Civil de Wicres is in English, as follows:—

The xvii. June, was baptized (the paper he parenthesises is torn at the spot of the Christian name) Du Bois, son of Chrétien. Godfather, Laurent Du Bois; Godmother, Heleine de Beaussart; (1622).

The xiii. November, was baptized (in parenthesis—the Christian name is torn out) Du Bois, son of Chrétien. Godfather, Jacques Du Bois, and Godmother, Rogeau (1625).

The xxi. October, was baptized To——(the rest illegible or torn out, he does not say which, but puts in parenthesis [probably Toussaint] Du Bois, son of Chrétien. Godfather, Franchois Du Bois (so pronounced), and Godmother, Catherine de Marsy (1626).

I would here remark that the *To* resembles *Lo* as much as To, and possibly may have been Louis, and the archivist thinking he made out *Touis*, knew of no French name like it but *Toussaint*. It is certain that Chrétien had a son Louis, and that he was born in October, 1626.

A previous record sent us by M. Du Bois Grégoire, as furnished him by the archivist, states that Chrétien Du Bois and his wife had a child, Louis Du Bois, *born* the 28th October, 1626.

The baptism just referred to is on the 21st October, 1626, of a son of Chrétien, of whose name only the first two letters are extant.

The explanation of the inconsistency, as reported, of a child that was born the 28th of the month, baptized the 21st of the month, is very simple. The Roman numerals, and not the Arabic, are used: xxviii. represents the birth as given, and xxi. the baptism as above given; but a previous letter gave the baptism of this child (with no name and no letters, T. O. or L. O., for a part of the name) as occurring October xxvii. (27th), 1626. This date, which lacks but the Roman numeral i. added to the vii., to make it correspond with the birth, is no doubt nearer the true date, and identifies the child with Louis. It was at that time an every-day occurrence to baptize a child on the day of its birth, or the day after. And in such old records, where the writing is scarcely decipherable, the exact birthday of the month, or the actual baptismal day of the month, represented by Roman numerals, may not be correctly made out in these extracts.

These three baptisms are all that occur in these records of the sons of Chrétien. But we know he had a daughter Françoise, and it seems he had a daughter Anne also; for on the 18th July, 1643, at the baptism of Jean Baptiste Du Bois, son of Franchois (so pronounced), and of Jeanne Marie Brunel, his Godmother is entered as Anne Du Bois, daughter of Chrétien Du Bois.

The same registers at Wicres record the births and baptisms of Anne, Albert, Jacqueline and Philip Du Bois, who were cousins of our Jacques Du Bois (this we know from the Leyden records). The Godfather of Jacqueline was a Jacques Du Bois, and he was also Godfather to a son of Chrétien, and that son was probably my ancestor, Jacques, named for his Godfather. Jacqueline, his cousin, was called after him. He stood for both. In that case, Jacques was Louis' elder brother, as M. Grégoire and his archivist seem to imagine to be the fact, and the eldest child of all, baptized in June, 1622, may have been the daughter, Françoise. The difference in the old manuscript between the French word "fils" (son) and "fille" (daughter) may have naturally escaped notice.

There is also in the same register a record of the baptism of four children of a Franchois Du Bois, viz: Anne in 1635, Franchois in 1639, Jean Baptiste in 1643 (to this child, Chrétien's daughter, Anne, stood sponsor), and Jaspar in 1645. All these Christian names seem to be easily made out, and it is only where Chrétien's children are registered that their first names are torn out. At least, from the letters of M. Grégoire, it would appear so.

It was a characteristic of the dialect spoken in the Walloon provinces to pronounce François, and to write it, Franchois, substituting the letters *c h* for c weak, or c with the sound of s.

The obliteration and destruction of all protestant family records in France, carried into effect by order of Louis XIV., who at the time of the expatriation of our forefathers was king of France, have rendered it impossible for the descendants of Huguenots to trace their family records in that country beyond the time of that monarch; and especially so, if they were in any way allied to a noble family, and in a possible line of succession to the estate. Not only were their lands and goods confiscated, but their very names were erased or torn out in baptismal and genealogical registers.

Louis was born in October, 1626; consequently he was a man grown before the first or any of these foregoing genealogies were discontinued. At the time of his marriage at Manheim, in 1655, his father's children had all fled from Artois.

Françoise, the sister of Louis, was at Leyden, in Holland, as early as April 20th, 1649, for she was on that day married there to Pierre Biljouw, in the church of the Walloons. The betrothal was registered in the town hall records, April 3d, 1649. The record states that both came from near Lille. La Bassée, Lille and Wicres are all near to each other.

Biljouw and his wife had two daughters born to them at Leyden. The elder, Marie, was baptized at Leyden, March 3d, 1650. She was afterwards married, at Kingston, in Ulster county, to Arendt Jansen, from Nardy. The contract of marriage, dated June 3d, 1670, specifies that her uncle, Louis Du Bois, affirms or ratifies the betrothal. This contract is still preserved among the old records of Ulster county.

At the baptism of his other niece, Martha, at Leyden, February 8th, 1652, Albert Du Bois (who, I told you, took the name of Van der Bosch, a cousin of Jacques) stood Godfather to her. It was then customary for very near relatives to officiate in that capacity. A relationship, therefore, between Albert and the mother, Françoise, involves a relationship between Jacques and Louis. Were they also cousins? or were they brothers?

Françoise, I have already said, was married at Leyden, in the year 1649; Louis at Manheim, in 1655; Jacques at Leyden, in 1663. They had then permanently left their native land. But the question will arise, Why did they go thus early into exile? The edict of Nantes was not then repealed.—That occurred in 1685.

The thirty years' war, which had in its battlefields embraced the Netherlands, was then at an end. It had closed the religious wars which had for near a century deluged Europe with blood; which had arrayed not only nation against nation, but individual against individual, in the most cruel and deadly strife; for then it was literally true, that a man's foes were of his own household. But these desolating wars had been brought to a close by the peace of Westphalia, in 1648. Why should they, then, immediately thereafter leave their homes and seek an asylum in other lands?

A reference to the treaty of peace, concluded at Osnabrück in 1648, will furnish the answer. Under it Calvinists and Lutherans were admitted to equal rights, Switzerland and the United Provinces of the Netherlands were declared independent, and there was to be freedom of conscience and religious toleration everywhere, *except in the Austrian dominions.*

Here we see the answer to that question, and the reason why our forefathers did at that time expatriate themselves. They fled at first to Holland, and eventually, under the guidance of a Divine Providence, they made for themselves a home beyond the seas.

They were not to be benefited in their native land by the peace. They were but too vividly reminded of the five thousand persons who in the Netherlands were put to death by that Austrian despot Charles V., for disobedience of his decree, called the "Interim," by hanging, burning, and burying alive. They remembered the thirteen new bishoprics that Pope Pius IV. had created among them for the purpose of stopping the spread of heresy. And they feared the Inquisition. They had heard of the *auto-da-fes* which Philip II., the son of the Austrian monarch, gloated on, while his subjects of the reformed religion were consuming in fire under his palace windows at Seville, and at his native Valladolid; and they realized the fact, with all its horrors to protestants, that Artois, their native land, was then under Austrian domination. The Philips of Spain were all of the Austrian dynasty, and therefore it was that our ancestors fled.

A brief glance at the origin of these persecutions, and I have done.

The suppressing of heresy was the motive seized upon by the reigning monarchs for measures which had for their real object the depriving of the people of all political power, and the keeping them under the iron bondage of an absolute monarchy.

Hugh Capet originated the policy in France of breaking down the power of the feudal lords, who, in many instances, as I have intimated, possessed a sovereign authority independent of and greater than that of the king himself. It was a work of time, but with the breaking up of the feudal system it was accomplished. When succeeding monarchs had attained this object, they took a lesson from the arrogant pretensions of the Pope of Rome. They came to believe that they too ruled by divine right, and that subjects had no civil rights but such as the sovereign might, of his own free will, accord to them.

As Thomas Hobbes, the philosopher of Malmesbury, inculcated in more recent times, so these kings believed, that the will of the sovereign should be the conscience of every good man. In this, you perceive, consists the real essence of popery. It was by teaching this doctrine to an ignorant people in the dark ages, that the Roman hierarchy had succeeded in enslaving Christendom, and in bringing even kings themselves into subjection to the Holy See. Upon this assumption, and by the aid of the confessional, they had built up a system of abject slavery, making the degraded people believe that their souls' salvation depended upon the absolution of the priest; and to obtain this they must observe the duties and external ceremonies imposed by the church.

The clergy were the depositories of all revealed and saving truth; but what that truth was, as taught in Scripture, they themselves did not know. They were perfectly ignorant of the essential character of God, as revealed in His Word and Works, and as still more plainly and perfectly manifested in the life and character and teaching of the adorable Son of God, coming to us in the flesh. They rather conceived of God as he was represented to the pagan mind and delineated in heathen mythology.

The monks, whose seclusion in cloisters gave them the leisure for study, and who alone made any pretensions to learning, were more given to the study of ancient philosophy than of the Bible They were impressed with the idea that the Platonic and Aristotelian philosophy and Christian theology were reconcilable, and their study was to reconcile them. Their endeavor was to apply the dialectics of Aristotle (a disbelief in whom was heresy) to the elucidation of traditional Christian dogmas. Thus arose the scholasticism of the middle ages, and a subtle and spiritualizing mode of reasoning on metaphysical ideas and abstract propositions subversive of all revealed truth and of the foundations of correct and sound reasoning. Arguments could readily be invented in support of the gross immorality of the papal court, and of the abominable licentiousness of the clergy.

With these excesses on the part of those claiming authority in sacred things, the moral sense of right and wrong implanted in the human breast was outraged. Councils were convened before Luther's day for the avowed object of reforming the church in its head and members. The contest began between kings and popes, which resulted in breaking off from royal necks the galling yoke of the Papal See. A tacit agreement, or compromise as it were, was however had between the temporal and spiritual aggressors, that the people should not be free. The spiritual bondage was to be strengthened by secular chains. In matters of religion as well as of government the people were to yield implicit obedience to the supreme will. God, in his wise and overruling providence, thus permitted the alliance of monarchical and spiritual despotism, that He might destroy both.

The principles of religious and civil freedom became involved in a common cause, and they who would never of their own accord have taken up arms to spread their religion, but who, like the early Christians, would have willingly submitted to persecution for conscience sake, and would have also taken joyfully the spoiling of their goods, knowing in themselves that they had in heaven a better and an enduring substance, were unavoidably compelled to shed the blood of their fellow-men in its defence in the wars of religion.

In the civil wars, which either the tyranny of the sovereign, the interference of the pontiff, or the strife of contending factions aiming at kingly power had engendered throughout all Europe, these peace-loving and law-abiding Christians were necessarily enlisted in long-protracted and cruel, bloody wars for the maintenance of civil rights and religious freedom.

It is true, the struggle was not a triumphant one for the Huguenots in France, who therefore had to flee the country, but it was successful in other parts of Europe, and especially in England and Holland. And this terrible contest, in which millions of lives were sacrificed, has indelibly impressed upon the civilized world at this day the lesson which was so difficult for despots to learn,—that the conscience of enlightened Christian men partakes as well of reason as of feeling.

My friends! the consciousness of duty was to our fathers an instinctive feeling. The perception of right and wrong was an operation of their understanding.

The Huguenots who were thus forced to leave their native land were an intelligent as well as a religious and a chivalric race. Wherever the light of the gospel had dispelled the darkness of mediæval times, there the hand of welcome was opened wide to receive them, for they brought with them industry, a knowledge of the mechanic arts, a determination that their own hands should minister to their necessities, and an elevating and refining Christian influence upon the communities which sheltered them. Such were our ancestors; and they have left to us, their descendants, a title of nobility far above the blazonry of heraldic arms, and of which alone we, as citizens of a free republic, should ever pride ourselves—and that title to public esteem and consideration is a descent from *Huguenot fathers*.

In the language of the poet Cowper (adapting his words to the plural number)—

"Our boast is not, that we deduce our birth
From loins enthroned, and rulers of the earth;
But higher far our proud pretensions rise,
The sons of parents past into the skies."

At the conclusion of this discourse, the doxology was sung and benediction pronounced, and the meeting adjourned for dinner.

Concerning this generous provision, the best we can do is to quote from the able reports of the newspapers. Thus the *Daily Freeman*, of Kingston*—

"Such as could remain were invited to partake of refreshments prepared in the lecture-room of the church, and thither a goodly number wended their way, surrounding the tables spread with a great abundance of good cheer, prepared by the fair and willing hands of the lady representatives of the Du Bois family and the New Paltz church.

* This is a good opportunity to mention, that elaborate reports of the meeting appeared in the two journals cited, as also in the New Paltz papers, while lesser accounts were given in others.

"The scene in the lecture-room was a very enlivening and interesting one. Every Du Bois had some other Du Bois by the button-hole or seated in cosy converse together. Groups of Du Boises talked and laughed here; frisky young Du Boises had a jollification in one corner; while their elders, more staid and quiet, soberly talked of by-gone days in another. The ladies had tastefully decorated the room. In large letters, formed of evergreens, three large mottoes were displayed, being respectively—

LOUIS DU BOIS.
WELCOME TO NEW PALTZ.
HUGUENOTS.
1675–1875.

"The pillars supporting the ceiling were twined about with leaves, and beautiful floral bouquets decorated the tables and made the air heavy with their fragrance. The good things were soon being actively circulated, and the masticating process was accompanied by the cheerful hum of conversation. Refreshments for four hundred guests had been prepared, and it is thought that about that number partook of them.

"Ample time was given to the enjoyments of the table, and then the company dispersed about the grounds and village to pass the time in each other's society, and await the bell summoning them to a resumption of the exercises."

And the *Hudson Star*—

"The hospitable inhabitants of New Paltz had, with deft and cunning hands, transformed the spacious room into a banquet hall, where, amid floral decorations on all sides, and with the air heavy with the fragrance of nature's offerings entwined around, tempting viands were spread out with a lavish hand."

On reassembling in the afternoon,

An appropriate anthem was sung by the well-trained choir of sixteen ladies and gentlemen of New Paltz, with instrumental accompaniment.

Prayer was offered by Rev. Dr. Richard De Witt.

The following paper, by Dr. Henry A. Du Bois,* who was too unwell to be present, was read by Gilbert Du Bois,† of Napanoch.

THE FAMILY SURNAME.

Fellow-kinsmen, Descendants of Louis and Jacques du Bois.

We have met here to commemorate our descent from two noble and pious men, who, more than two hundred years ago, fled from persecution in their native land, and found an asylum in this place, then a wilderness.

Peeled and stripped, for conscience sake, in the old world, they brought with them to this new world but few earthly possessions; but they came rich in a *pure* faith, and endowed with indomitable courage and energy to maintain it. This precious legacy they have bequeathed to a numerous posterity, of the seventh and eighth generations; and though few of them may have achieved much worldly distinction, I have yet to learn the name of that one who, by dishonor or by dishonesty, has sullied his family patronymic. Other members of the family have undertaken to portray the lives of these two pious refugees, especially of Louis, the older brother—to describe their hardships and trials in the wilderness, their progress from poverty to comparative wealth, the influence which they exerted on the community which sprang up around them on both sides of the Hudson, the general characteristics of the race, and the dispersion of their numerous descendants and their settlement in other parts.

To my brother has been assigned the task of giving the history of the du Bois family in France and Holland. I propose to make the *name itself* the theme of this short address.—"What's in a name?" Juliet asked, and Romeo might have answered with great truth, "A great deal, since a name separates us." So we

* This gentleman, residing at New Haven, Conn., is Doctor of Medicine and of Laws; not a practising physician. He is known as the author of several reviews, chiefly on subjects of science as bearing upon religion, which have been highly commended, both in America and England. His house is doubly Huguenot, as he married into the Jay family. He is brother of Cornelius and George W., already mentioned.

† Of this well-known citizen of Ulster, president of the Ellenville Bank, we shall have repeated occasion to speak. [EDS.]

DvBois

also may reply, a great deal, since a name unites us all as kindred in America, and allies us to a very ancient and noble stock in Europe. This point I will now proceed to prove.

Ancient family surnames, which have been transmitted unaltered from generation to generation, indicate with great certainty a common origin on the part of all those who have rightfully inherited such ANCIENT surnames.

The family name which these two refugees bore is a peculiar one, and is probably the most ancient name now extant. Written in the form in which they and their predecessors, for six hundred years, invariably wrote it, viz: with a small "d" and a capital "B," it was an incontestable badge of noble extraction, though the possessor, by adverse circumstances, might have been degraded from rank into the lower levels of society. Abjuring the Romish faith would be inevitably visited with such degradation, and the name erased from the parish and family records. There are several instances on record of some of this name who, after degradation, had been restored, and, as the record expresses it, "réhabilités en noblesse."

I have not the ability, if I had the wish, to trace the descent of these pious men from "loins enthroned or rulers of the earth," for they have a far higher heraldry in the skies; but a few remarks in regard to the antiquity of this family name will, I trust, prove interesting to those who have inherited it.

According to Père Anselme, de Laignes, and other learned genealogists, there were at first no fixed family names in Europe outside of the nobility. After the year 1339, wealthy families, not noble, assumed and transmitted family names derived from lands acquired or inherited.

Among industrial classes of society, fixed surnames did not exist till long afterwards. These are of comparatively recent origin, and were first assumed as indicative of parentage or occupation, such as Johnson, Peterson, Nicholson, Thompson, etc., or Mason, Carpenter, Tailor, Glover, Wainwright, Baker, Brewer, etc., *ad infinitum*. Such names are still in process of formation, especially amongst the Teutonic race landing on our shores.

But all the *ancient* family surnames which can be traced back *prior to the year one thousand two hundred*, are, according to the above authors, of noble origin.

Previous to the year 900, no fixed family surnames existed in France, even amongst the nobles. At this time barons and knights held their lands as revocable gifts from sovereign princes, secular or ecclesiastical. But after 987, they began to acquire possession of their lands in hereditary fee, paying only feudal service to their *suzerains*. At this time, therefore, these barons and knights first began to transmit their family names, as well as their lands, to their posterity, and the name of an estate, inherited or acquired by marriage, was generally affixed to the original surname to distinguish the different branches of the same family.

Of these ancient patronymics, probably the *most ancient* one which has descended unchanged to this time, is that of "du Bois."

After consulting all the oldest genealogical authors and books of heraldry in the ancient Bibliotheque du Roi (now Bibliotheque Nationale), at Paris, I found but one name which is now extant of equal antiquity.*—This is the name of "Pierrepont," which, like that of "du Bois," has come down for many centuries to the present time unaltered in a single letter.

The origin of both these ancient family surnames was derived from hereditary office. Père Anselme and Dufourny, in the eighth folio volume of their great work, entitled "Maison Royale de France," at pages 865 to 869, speak of the family "du Bois" as the "Grand Masters of the Forests of France," and of the family "Pierrepont" as the "Grand Masters of the Waters of France."

The above authors attribute a common origin to both these ancient families, to wit: from Macquaire du Bois, Count de Roussy, in 1110, whose ancestor built the Castle de Roussy in 948, and added this title to his patronymic. Macquaire's son was Hugh de Roussy, surnamed "le Cholet," whose fourth son, not succeeding to the titles, perpetuated the line under the title of "Seigneurs du Bois de Marne," for fifteen generations, when Guillaume du Bois, in 1484, took the title of de Roussy. The great-grandson of Hughes du Bois perpetuated the line of the "Seigneurs de Pierrepont" for twelve generations, when both branches, according to this record, took the name of de Roussy.

* Dr. Schenck has traced *his* to the eighth century. (EDS.)

The Castle of de Roussy was situated in Artois, where some suppose the name of "du Bois" to have originated Other genealogical authors trace the origin of this family name to that part of France anciently called Neustria, a part of which was afterwards known as Normandy. It evidently existed there as an old name before the Norwegian Rollo, with his band of Norman followers, invaded that ancient province of France, and became the first duke of Normandy.

M. de Saint Allais, in his "Nobiliare de France," speaks of this name as that of one of the most ancient of the noble families of Normandy. He traces one of its branches, namely, that of "du Bois du Bais," from 1066 (at which time it was an old family), down to the present century, by regular descent from father to son, the original patronymic being unchanged throughout. All the authors on historic genealogy concur in mentioning this surname as belonging to very ancient families in other parts of France, especially in Artois, Flanders and Brittany; but all bearing this patronymic are supposed to have had a common origin.

During my recent sojourn in Paris, I visited the Viscount de Magny, the present head of the Heraldic College of France, and had several conversations and some correspondence with him. He said to me: "Your family name, 'du Bois,' is one of the very oldest in France, and has more extensive marriage connections than any other." He writes: "I have some three hundred manuscript documents in regard to it." It is divided, according to him, into five principal branches, which exist in different parts of France, in Flanders, and even in England, but all these branches are traceable (he thinks) to a common origin in Normandy.

A few words in regard to the *orthography* of this ancient name will be appropriate and interesting to those who bear it. In many hundred instances in which I have examined this name in various books of heraldry, I have never but in one instance found it written otherwise than with a small "d" and with a capital "B,"—thus, "du Bois." The exception was in the case of a woman incidentally mentioned, and the reason not explained.

The prefix to a family name of "de," "de la," or of "du," which is a contraction of "de le," is universally admitted in France to be a badge of noble extraction.

While living in France, forty years ago, I made the acquaintance of M. Dumas, a near relative of the author. One day he said to me, "Do you sign your name with a large 'B' or a small 'b?'" I told him that my father and all his predecessors invariably signed their names with a capital B, but that I wrote it indifferently both ways, as I supposed it was the same name. He replied, "You are quite mistaken. If you have the *right* to sign your name with a large 'B,' you belong to an ancient French family, of which there are now but few representatives." "But," he added, "there are great numbers in the south and middle of France who write this name with a small 'b,' and who are of an entirely different origin. These were probably the descendants of the enfranchised peasantry or serfs who, in migrating to other parts, took the name of their feudal lords, but without the badge which indicated noble extraction, as this, in France, would have been a penal offence on their part. Thus the talented but infamous Cardinal Dubois never dared to write his name with a capital 'B,' for during his day there were many powerful branches of the noble family 'du Bois' jealous of their hereditary patronymic, who would have immediately impleaded him before the parliament of France, and have convicted him of imposture."

Louis and Jacques du Bois were the first who brought this ancient name to the new world, and they wrote it as it was invariably written six hundred years previously, with a small "d" and a capital "B."

At the present time their direct lineal descendants exist in the seventh and eighth generation. All these descendants have always signed their names with a capital "B," after the example of their respective progenitors, but they should also have written the prefix "du," as they wrote it, and not with a capital "D."

It is very desirable that all the descendants of Louis and Jacques du Bois should maintain their family patronymic intact as a badge of their common origin, and write it in the same way that their forefathers did. This would not necessitate the change of a single letter, but simply a return to the ancient usage of writing the first letter of the prefix "du" with a small "d."

This uniformity in writing the name I strenuously advocate, not only as an indication of descent from these two noble champions of protestantism who first brought it to this country, but also as a distinction from French citizens now settling in our midst, whose names, though apparently similar, are *essentially* different, and who are of a different lineage, and also of a different and adverse faith.

I am no advocate for nobiliary titles—still less for nobiliary privileges. Such pretensions are inconsistent with the simplicity of the republican institutions bequeathed to us by our revolutionary fathers. Still more abhorrent would they be to the prevailing ochlocratic spirit of the present day, which has superseded our old republican principles, and is fast degrading, if not destroying, all that our forefathers esteemed virtuous and respectable. But to every right-minded man it must be a subject of just and honest pride to be descended from a long line of pious ancestors in this country, even though he should be reproached for claiming descent from a noble stock in Europe.

Fellow-kinsmen, the time is fast approaching when we will be called upon to maintain those principles of civil and religious liberty which our forefathers planted in this country, and which are now menaced by the same foe which persecuted them.

Rome has at this day, and in this country, far more political and spiritual power than she has in any country in Europe, and more than she had in France under Louis XIV., when she drove our ancestors from their native land. She then sought to obtain her ends by the aid of a royal despot: she now finds a more powerful ally in demagogism, which is and always has been the bane of all free institutions.

In the impending struggle for an unimpaired national life which looms up in the near future, I predict that all the descendants of the two noble Huguenot refugees, Louis and Jacques du Bois, will be found battling on the side of patriotism, intelligence and religious freedom, against ignorance, superstition and demagogism upheld by the subtle craft and wily politics of Rome.

Among the earliest and very best settlers of this country, the Huguenots stand foremost as a race. Wherever they settled, north or south, they have ever been noted as virtuous and useful citizens, honorable men, and fearless upholders of civil and religious liberty. Of these Huguenots, one of the most ancient families is that of "du Bois." For more than two hundred years they have maintained in this country their family name unsullied.

Let us, therefore, fellow-kinsmen, reverence our American progenitors, Louis and Jacques, not for their claims to ancient lineage in the old world, but for the piety, courage and honorable principles which they have transmitted to their descendants in the new world.

The President read the following paper, on

THE LIFE AND TIMES OF LOUIS DU BOIS.*

I am to present to you a sketch of the life and times of Louis Du Bois (called sometimes Louis de Wall, or the Walloon), from the date of his arrival in America. We have just had what can be known of his European history; his birth at Wicres, near Lille, the chief town of Artois, in northern France, October 27th, 1626; his retiring to the city of Mannheim, in the Palatinate of the Rhine, in Germany, where he married Catherine Blanshan, or Blanjean, the daughter of a burgher of that place, October 10th, 1655; and the birth there of two sons, Abraham and Isaac. This little family, doubtless with other French protestants, embarked for America in 1660, seeking in the new world, an asylum from royal and Romish persecution. They sailed, no doubt, from a Holland port, in a Dutch vessel, to these western possessions of the States-General. At the period in which they arrived, the whole country was new. How different the bay of New York, upon which our ancestors looked in 1660, and the same bay at the present time! And still greater changes have taken place on Manhattan Island. Then Wall street and Broadway inclosed the quaint, irregularly-built little town, nestled upon the lower point of the island sloping to the East river, and even this narrow extent broken by sandhills, marshy meadows and broad, open ditches. Two hundred poorly constructed houses gave partial comfort to some fourteen hundred people. The fort

* The writer and reader of this article, Anson Du Bois, is of the tribe of Benjamin, who was a son of Solomon, son of Louis. They belong to Catskill. He was formerly pastor of the Second Reformed Church in Kingston; now of the Reformed Church of Flatlands, near Brooklyn.

loomed up broadly in front, partially hiding within it the barracks, the governor's official residence, and the Old Dutch church. A globe-shaped steeple upon the latter seemed to suggest that the church alone could elevate the world, and the weathercock, upon his high perch, stood watching for the millenial morning. The flag of the States-General, and a wind-mill on the western bastion, were notable indications of Hollandish rule. Wherever else in all that broad and beautiful bay, the eye of our ancestor rested, he saw only the forest, with possibly here and there an opening among the trees.

We have not the name of the ship or of his fellow-passengers. Probably Rev. Henricus Selyns, afterwards pastor at Brooklyn, and his companion to America, Rev. Hermanus Blom, were in the company. Blom had preached at Kingston the previous year and now came to settle there, and thus became the pastor of Louis Du Bois. They came in the same year, but we cannot say that they came in the same ship. Mathew Blanshan, a brother-in-law, and Antoni Crispel and Hugo Frere, early and intimate friends of Louis, may also have been with him.

Du Bois and his companions must have landed at the company's dock, some two blocks from South ferry, near Moore street. Turning to the left, they would have passed the White Hall of Governor Stuyvesant and the fort, and entered the *Heere straat* —the "Lord street," or street of rank, now Broadway—just above Bowling Green. A little further up they would have found the substantial residence of the Dutch clergyman, or dominie, as the Dutch delight to call him, Rev. —— Megapolensis. Just across the street was the affable inn-keeper, Captain Martin Kregier, a man of mark, a captain of the militia, a burgomaster, and officer of the council. His discretion and bravery had full exercise three years after this, while in command at Esopus.

Du Bois may have met other refugees, some of whom came as early as 1628, and he may have found friends at New Rochelle.

Du Bois and his companions must now leave New Amsterdam. Governor Stuyvesant was absent on business, in the summer of 1660, at Esopus and Fort Orange; if his absence occurred at this time, Du Bois applied for permission to go to the upper country to Henrick Van Dyck, the schout fischael, whose tasteful mansion stood on the Heere straat, among gardens and orchards, running down to the North river, and near Dominie Megapolensis.

All things being in readiness, Du Bois, with his wife, children and friends, much refreshed by their sojourn in the city, set out for the upper Hudson. The scenes were now a constant wonder to people who had sailed only on European rivers, where hamlet and castle and city leave scarcely room for farm or garden. The sloping eastern shore, the bald front of the Palisades, the Highlands, with narrower water, and towering peaks springing to the clouds from either shore; the broader bay at Newburg, and, finally, the blue outlines of the Shawangunk and the Catskills, met their gaze. Everywhere were forests, vast and deep. At long intervals only could be seen the thin smoke of the Indian wigwam circling among the tree-tops, or a bark-canoe gliding furtively across some darksome bay; but nothing, in the long, tedious sail, that bore the most distant resemblance to their old home beyond the Atlantic.

We must suppose that deep, earnest thoughts crowded themselves upon the active mind of our ancestor in that voyage up the Hudson. Everything so new, strange and bewildering. The sky only, of all about him, remained unchanged, and the stars at night; and as he looked on these he felt that Heaven beyond them and his divine Lord and Saviour were unchanged and unchangeable. He had fled from country and kindred for God and liberty. This wilderness was to be his home and that of his children. He could not forecast the future, but one thing was sure—he knew in whom he had believed, and could trust all to Him.

At length the sloop turned her prow into the Rondout creek. The village of Wiltwyck, in the "Esopus country," as Dominie Blom designated the Kingston of his day, was now just beginning its permanent growth. History states that the Dutch established a trading post at Rondout in 1614. Tradition, however, has it that the first settlers of Ulster county landed at Saugerties, and followed up the Esopus kill, through unbroken forests, twelve miles, and settled finally at Kingston, being attracted by the rich alluvial meadows. But this settlement was twice broken up before the arrival of our emigrants, and so late as

1655 is said to have been wholly abandoned. Before 1660 it had been reoccupied and put in some posture of defence.

We have now conducted Louis Du Bois and his associates to their first American home. We must narrate their labors at this place, and the terrible events through which they were led, all of which show the character of our Huguenot ancestors, and have important relation to the history of New Paltz.

Soon after arriving at Wiltwyck, we may suppose Louis Du Bois took measures for securing a home and a portion of land; for he had been a tiller of the soil, and, like the Old Testament patriarchs, "his trade hath been about cattle." We have commonly assumed that his home was at Wiltwyck, now Kingston, before going to New Paltz. This is probably incorrect. His home at this period was at Hurley, three miles from Kingston, where he kept a store and traded thriftily with his neighbors and the people of the back settlements, and with the Indians. At the Indian raid of 1663, Hurley was almost entirely destroyed. Here the Indians secured most of the captives, and amongst them the wife and three children of Du Bois, as will appear hereafter.

And now Louis and his Christian friends join heart and hand in the work of the church, which had been organized, however, in 1659—before their arrival.

Let me hastily trace the ever-widening stream from this early opened fountain. The first effort was to build a house of worship. It was a rude affair of logs, and upon the lot now occupied by the stately edifice of the First Reformed Church of Kingston. This building remained until 1679, and was occupied during the ministry of Hermanus Blom, Peter Tessemaker, and Laurentius Van Gaasbeek. A second building was completed in 1680, a few weeks after the death of Dominie Van Gaasbeek. This church was in the ancient style, with highly colored window-glass, bearing the coat-of-arms of the principal families; (this glass was made and painted in New York by Evert Duykinck, and was set by his son Gerrit, who came up for the purpose.) A third was erected in 1721, and the same enlarged in 1752. In 1777, October 16th, the church was burnt, with the village. It was rebuilt upon the old walls, after the revolution, and this remained, the ornament of the village and the centre of religious influences, until 1833, when the time-honored and noble structure yielded to a spirit of destruction, and the brick church, on the opposite side of the street, was erected,—now, unhappily, surrendered to the Romanists.

The congregation worshipped in the brick church until September 21st, 1853, when they entered their present large and handsome edifice. This was the mother-church in this region. If Louis Du Bois and his co-laborers could have foreseen the fruits of their toil in this section of the country, they would indeed have been like those who "foresaw the day of Christ, and were glad."

There seem to have been a number of Huguenot settlers in Wiltwyck and vicinity, commingled with the Dutch. The records of baptisms and marriages kept by the ministers were in Dutch, but it is an interesting fact, that the records of the Kingston church were kept in the French tongue until some years after 1700. Though the preaching was doubtless mainly in Dutch, yet the Huguenot membership and influence was very considerable. A satisfactory peace had been concluded with the Esopus Indians, and prosperity now attended the settlement. The lands in the neighborhood were successfully cultivated, and hamlets formed at Hurley and Marbletown. The village increased in importance.

Good Dominie Blom saw prosperity attend his spiritual labors,* his membership increasing from sixteen to sixty within three years.

But peace was the exception, not the rule, in those early times. The Indians were jealous and inimical, and, unfortunately for the good name of civilization and Christianity, as has been the case often since, were not without just cause of offence. After the conclusion of peace, the director-general was so impolitic—to use no severer word—as to transport *eleven Indians* to Curaçoa, where formerly he had been governor, to be sold as slaves. Under what pretext this outrage was committed we do not know, but the consequences were very serious. The Indians

* At the date of 1665, there were fifty-five holders of pews, and Louis Du Bois paid thirteen guilders a year for pew-rent.

naturally determined on revenge, and from the fact that the Esopus country was made the seat of war, it is probable that the enslaved Indians were of that tribe, while there is proof that the other tribes, and especially those further south, sympathized with them.

The particulars of this war, which is called the "Second Esopus War," are fully given in Doc. Hist. N. Y., vol. iv. We are especially interested in it, because Louis Du Bois and his family were among the sufferers. The little town of Wiltwyck had no suspicion of the impending storm. The stockade was in a dilapidated condition, and the fort nearly incapable of defence, though a few soldiers still lingered about it. The Indians had just been invited by the Director-General to meet him, and renew the peace, and they gave no indication of unwillingness to do so. The people were scattered about, at their various occupations in town and field. In this condition of affairs, on June 7th, 1663, the Indians entered within the stockade, and, under various pretexts, scattered themselves through the town. Suddenly, near noon, a horseman dashed through the Mill gate, now corner of North Front and Greene, crying, "The Indians have destroyed the New Village"—that is, Hurley. This was the signal for the slaughter. The tomahawk and the musket did their dreadful work. The torch was applied at the windward of the village; the smoke rolled over the terrified people, who could not know how to strike their enemies, or protect their own lives and families. Some fled to the fort, others fired from their houses, or met the foe bravely, hand to hand, in the streets. Shots in rapid succession, screams, groans, the mother's cry and the child's answer, the loud calls of the men as they concerted some plan of defence, and the bloody work of the savages followed! Many a scream ended suddenly by the heavy thud of the war-club. The women, helpless to fight or flee, were herded together with the children, and driven outside the gates. It was an extreme moment, for courage and carnage were not wanting. Those in the town, under Captain Thomas Chalmers, acted a noble part, and he, though wounded and constantly under fire, soon rallied the available force of the village. The sheriff and commissaries were fully equal to the emergency, and even Dominie Blom was among the bravest in this terrific blast of savage warfare. There seem not to have been above *twenty* available men. "By these men," says the account, "most of whom had neither guns nor side-arms, were the Indians, through God's mercy, chased and put to flight. By a special favor of Providence, the wind changed when the flames were at their height, and spared the village from complete destruction."

We do not know where Louis DuBois was during the time of the Indian raid upon Wiltwyck. It is possible that he was engaged in the field at too great a distance to return until the fight was over. Or, if his residence was at or near Hurley, his absence is easily accounted for. We have every reason to know that his courage and physical strength would have aided greatly in resisting the savages, had he been present. A special instance of his prowess and presence of mind may be quoted from Captain Kregier's account, which of itself is sufficient proof of what we say:—

"Louis, the Walloon, went to-day to fetch his oxen, which had gone back of Juriaen Westphaelen's land. As he was about to drive home the oxen, three Indians, who lay in the bush and intended to seize him, leaped forth. When one of these shot at him with an arrow, but only slightly wounded him, Louis, having a piece of palisade in his hand, struck the Indian on the breast with it, so that he staggered back, and Louis escaped through the kill (creek)."

A man who, even when wounded, could overpower three armed Indians surprising him from an ambush, and escape them, was a man to be missed in the bloody mêlée that swept through the shivering streets of Wiltwyck.

But though the ruthless enemy had been driven out, and the gates shut against them, the scenes within were most distressing. Says an account, written at the time: "There lay the burnt and slaughtered bodies, together with those wounded by bullets and axes. The last agonies and lamentations of many were dreadful to hear." "The dead lay as sheaves behind the mower." Outside the walls, were not only the enemy, but with them the captive wives and children. It did not avail them that the gates were hastily closed, or that their husbands and brothers and sons came hurrying in from the fields, so that by evening the town was safe from further attack. A dreadful captivity of shame and suffering was before them, and perhaps death itself.

Among the captives were the wife and three children of Louis Du Bois. We may imagine their terror and distress as their merciless captors drove them forward through the forests. They knew not who lay dead in the half-burnt town, or what terrible fate awaited them. In that captive company were one man, twelve married women, and thirty-one children. All of the women were mothers with their children, except one, who had been but lately married, and was driven from her young husband, each ignorant of the other's fate. Ten children were there without father or mother. These captives remained among the Indians for three months. They were separated from each other, and were constantly removed from place to place to avoid rescue. Some were in charge of old squaws, others were held in particular families, and others still were required to accompany the Indians in their wanderings through the country. At Wiltwyck, desolation and fear reigned. The first thought was to repair the fort and stockades. Pastor Blom, who had entered with such energy into the material conflict, remembered, soon after that conflict was fully over, that his office was especially to pour into wounded hearts the oil and wine of Christian consolation. "I have been in their midst" (of the dying), he says, "and have gone into their houses and along the roads to speak a word in season, and not without danger of being shot by the Indians. But I went on my mission, and considered not my life my own." Noble words! He adds: "I have also every evening, during a whole month, offered up prayer with the congregation on the four points of our fort, under the blue sky." The church seems not to have been burnt. We have a list of twelve houses destroyed, while the church is not mentioned.

Now follows in the little settlement a period of distressing anxiety. The terrors of an Indian war were upon them,—a foe that could spring out of the dark forest suddenly, as the lightning from the black clouds. The first care, after guarding the town, was to send to New York for help. On June 16th, Lieut. Christian Nyssen arrived with forty-two soldiers, and on July 4th came our old friend Captain Martin Kregier, and a larger force in two yachts, and ample military supplies. But the poor captive women and children were not to be rescued in a day. The summer passed in negotiating with the Indians for their return, and in guarding the gathering of the harvest.

We cannot suppose that Louis Du Bois was all this time unconcerned about the situation of his family. He prayed often, but he expected no miraculous deliverance of the long-lost captives. How gladly, then, he hailed the prospect of some efficient means for their restoration! The attempt was prepared for early in September. A strong detachment of military, of which Captain Kregier had chief command, was to invade the Indian country. Information was carefully gleaned from friendly Indians, and from one or two escaped captives. A captured Wappinger Indian was employed to guide the rescuing party, having promise of his freedom and a cloth coat if he led them aright, but death in case of treachery. The place where the captives were held was the "New Fort," six miles from the junction of the Shawangunk kill with the Wall kill. The "Old Fort" was on the Kerhonksen, in Wawarsing. The Indian instructed the party of whites to ascend the first big water (Rondout) to where it received the second (Wall kill); then ascend the second big water to the third (Shawangunk), and near its mouth they would find the Indian stronghold. Here the party set out from Fort Wiltwyck September 3d. There were but forty-five men, all told, under Captain Kregier, with eight horses, taken for the bearing of the wounded. In the company, besides the soldiers and two negro slaves, were *seven freemen.* We have no record of their names. They were volunteers. We know, however, that Louis Du Bois was one of the number, and others may have been his brother-in-law, Mathew Blanshan, his intimate friends Antoine Crispell and Jan Joosten, who stood witnesses at the baptism of some of his children, and whose wives and children were captives. And may we not think that among the seven were Martin Harmansen, who had lost a wife and four children, and Joost Ariaens, whose young bride, Fennetje, had been ruthlessly torn from his embrace?

This rescuing party pressed on its rough way with their Wappinger Indian guide, and Christofful Davids as interpreter, and on the 5th of September they reached the vicinity of the New Fort. The following is Captain Kregier's account:—

"September 5th. Arrived, about two o'clock in the afternoon, within sight of their fort, which we discovered situated upon a lofty plain. Divided our force in two; Lieutenant Couwenhóven and I led the right wing, and Lieutenant Stilwill and Ensign Niessen the left wing. Proceeded, in this disposition, along the hill so as not to be seen, and in order to come right under the fort; but as it was somewhat level on the left side of the fort, and the soldiers were seen by a squaw who was piling wood there, and who sent forth a terrible scream which was heard by the Indians who were standing and working near the fort, we instantly fell upon them. The Indians rushed forthwith through the fort towards their houses, which stood about a stone's throw from the fort, in order to secure their arms, and thus hastily picked up a few guns and bows and arrows; but we were so hot at their heels that they were forced to leave many of them behind. We kept up a sharp fire upon them, and pursued them so closely that they leaped into the creek which ran in front of the lower part of their maize land. On reaching the opposite side of the kill, they courageously returned our fire, which we sent back, so that we were obliged to send a party across to dislodge them. In this attack the Indians lost their chief, named Japequanchen, fourteen other warriors, four women and three children, whom we saw lying both on this and on the other side of the creek; but probably many more were wounded when rushing from the fort to the houses, when we did give them a brave charge. On our side, three were killed and six wounded; and we have recovered three-and-twenty Christians, prisoners, out of their hands. We have also taken thirteen of them prisoners, both men and women.

"The fort was a perfect square, with one row of palisades set all round, being about fifteen feet above and three feet under ground. They had already completed two angles of stout palisades, all of them almost as thick as a man's body, having two rows of portholes, one above the other; and they were busy at the third angle. These angles were constructed so solid and so strong as not to be excelled by Christians. The fort was not so large as the one we had already burned. The Christian prisoners informed us that they were removed every night into the woods, each night into a different place, through fear of the Dutch, and brought back in the morning. But on the day before we attacked them, a Mohawk visited them, who slept with them during the night. When they would convey the Christian captives again into the woods, the Mohawk said to the Esopus Indians,—'What! Do you carry the Christian prisoners every night into the woods?' To which they answered, 'Yes.' Whereupon the Mohawk said, 'Let them remain at liberty here; for you live so far in the woods that the Dutch will not come hither, for they cannot come so far without being discovered before they reach you.' Wherefore they kept the prisoners by them that night. The Mohawk departed in the morning for the Manessings, and left a new blanket and two pieces of cloth, which fell to us also as booty; and we came just that day, and fell on them so that a portion of them is entirely annihilated."

In this historical recital, we have followed authentic documents. But there is a history among us for which we are not dependent on the State archives. The traditions of these early times have been preserved with remarkable clearness among the descendants of Louis Du Bois. Most of them I have myself heard many times from my grandfather and great-uncle. We associate them with the historical narrative already given, and we think correctly. The approach of the rescuing party at the New Fort was betrayed by their dogs, which ran on in advance and entered the Indian camp. The cry was at once raised and repeated, "*Swanekers and deers*," "White man's dogs," and thus the stealthy approach was betrayed. (This jargon, *swanekers and deers*, with its translation—white man's dogs—has been preserved among us for two centuries, wholly by tradition. You may imagine, therefore, how much I was interested in discovering lately, by cotemporaneous documents, that the word "*swanekers*" was the Indian word for "white man" among the Long Island Indians. In this instance our tradition is verified.)

It is also said, that as the whites neared the fort Louis Du Bois pressed on ardently, and perhaps incautiously, in advance. Thus exposed, an Indian, from behind a tree, was about to draw his bow for the fatal shot. But, for some cause, the arrow did not rest upon the bow-string, and Du Bois instantly sprang upon him with the agility and strength of a lion, and despatched him with his sword. One tradition has it that Du Bois ran him through with such force that the sword entered a log, and had to be withdrawn by placing his foot upon the prostrate body, and thus jerking it away by main strength!

"After this," says the account given in the Du Bois *Family Record*, "a consultation was held as to what course it was best to pursue. They agreed to wait till the dusk of the evening, that they might not be discovered at a distance, and then to rush upon them with a loud shout, as though a large force were coming to attack them, rightly judging that the Indians would flee, and leave their prisoners behind. The savages were engaged in preparations for the slaughter of one of their prisoners, and that none other than the wife of Du Bois. She had been placed on a pile of wood, on which she was to be burned to death. For her consolation, she had engaged in singing psalms, which having excited the attention of the Indians, they urged her by signs to resume her singing. She did so, and fortunately continued till the arrival of her friends. In good time her deliverers came. The alarm of their approach was given by the cry of 'White man's dogs—white man's dogs;' for while they were listening to the singing of their wives, the dogs had gone on and entered the encampment. They raised a shout. The Indians fled, and, strange as it may seem, the prisoners also fled with them; but Du Bois, being in advance and discovering his wife running after the Indians, he called her by name, which soon brought her to her friends. Having recovered the prisoners, they returned in safety by the way which they went.

"The recovered captives informed their husbands that they were soon to be sacrificed to savage fury, and that they had prolonged their lives by singing for their captors, and were just then singing the beautiful psalm of the 'Babylonish Captives,' when they heard the welcome sound of their deliverers' voices."

The following, from William E. Du Bois, will here be interesting:—

"In the psalmody of the French protestants, every psalm in French version and metre had its own tune; and not only the words, but the music written on the stave, were to be found in their books of devotion or appended to their printed Bibles. In a folio copy of the French Bible, printed at Amsterdam, the writer has found the music and words of this very psalm, the 137th, undoubtedly the same as was sung by Catherine Du Bois on this extraordinary occasion, and touchingly adapted to the very circumstances of the captives. The reader will allow us first to quote a part of the psalm as it stands in our English Bible, and then to add the corresponding verses of the French, as it was sung. As to the music, it is a slow, plaintive chant, in the minor mode, beautifully adapted to the subject. It is not in accordance with the style of our modern church music; but those who have listened to the sacred music in French protestant churches (undoubtedly the same as was used centuries ago), will agree with the writer, that it delightfully harmonizes with the solemnity and elevation of Christian worship. The following is our English version:* 'By the river of Babylon, there we sat down; yea, we wept when we remembered Zion,' &c., &c."

These psalms were much in use among the Huguenots, and they had been forbidden to sing them where they could be heard by others. These very words she had sung doubtless many times in suppressed tones, when hunted by ruthless persecutors and in peril of imprisonment and death. She had sung them in her voluntary exile from kindred and country, when her husband, her babe and religious faith were her only comforts. But now she sung them

* The following is the French version as she sang it :—

Etans assis aux rives aquatiques de Babilon,
Pleurions melancholiques,
Nous souvenans du pays de Sion,
Et au milieu de l' habitation,
Où de regrets tant de pleure épandîmes
Aux saules verts nos harpes nous pendîmes.
Lors ceux qui lá captifs nous emmenérent,
De les sonner fort nous importunérent,
Et de Sion les chansons reciter.
Las! dîmes nous, qui pourroit inciter
Nos tristes cœurs á chanter la loüange
De nôtre Dieu en un terre étrange.

with the joy of a believer about to die. Her singing proves her both a Christian and a courageous woman.

The rescue included the greater part of the captives. The Esopus tribe was now nearly exterminated. Late in the autumn they sued for peace,—which was established. The rich alluvial lands of the Wallkill Valley had attracted the favorable attention of the rescuing party. The results were of the most important character. Within three years of the rescue, May, 1666 (according to Edmund Eltinge), the purchase from the Indians of a large tract of land was effected by Louis Du Bois and his associates. The extent of this tract is differently stated. Mr. Eltinge makes it 144 square miles, or 92,160 acres. Rev. Dr. Stitt says: "It was an alluvial valley, beginning at Rosendale, bounded on the west by the Shawangunk mountains, and running as far south as a point called Gertrude's Nose (which overlooks the town of Shawangunk), and stretching from these two points in parallel lines to the Hudson river." Mr. Gilbert Du Bois estimates the tract to contain 36,000 acres. "The whole river line was about ten miles in length. On the southern border it extended westward, by a right line, about the same length to a conspicuous and immovable landmark, the 'Paltz Point.' * * * The northern boundary was seven miles long, the western five miles." Still another authority makes the southern line about twenty-one miles in length. I am disposed to think this latter correct. "The tract included part of the present townships of New Paltz, Rosendale and Esopus, and the whole of Lloyd." Highland has since been formed out of it.

The price paid was forty kettles, forty axes, forty adzes, forty shirts, four hundred strings of white beads (wampum), three hundred strings of black beads, fifty pairs of stockings, one hundred bars of lead, one keg of powder, one hundred knives, four quarter casks of wine, forty jars, sixty splitting or cleaving knives, sixty blankets, one hundred needles, one hundred awls and one clean pipe.

It was necessary that this transaction should be confirmed by the colonial government, and accordingly a patent deed was procured from Gov. Andross, September 29th, 1677, conveying to "Louis Du Bois and partners" the territory described, for the annual rent of "five bushels of good wheat"—a mere expression of acknowledgment to the lord paramount.

That important document, or rather a French translation of it, has been again translated by Mr. Wm. E. Du Bois, and is as follows:—

[TRANSLATION.]

Edmond Andross, Esquire, Lord of Saumarez, Lieutenant-Governor-General under his Royal Highness, James, Duke of York, of Albany, and of all his territories in America :—

WHEREAS, There is a certain piece of land at Esopus, which, by my approbation and consent, has been acquired from the Indian proprietors by Louis Du Bois and his associates; the said land being situated on the south side of the redoubt called Creek or Kill, being from [*i. e.* beginning at] the high mountain called Maggonck; thence extending from the southwest side, near the Great River, to a certain point or hook, called the Jauffrouc hook, situated along the tract called by the Indians Magaatramis, and from the north side ascending along the river to a certain island which makes an elbow at the beginning of the tract called by the Indians Raphoos; from the west side of the high mountains to the place called Waratakac and Tauarataque, and continues along the high mountains from [on?] the southwest side to Maggonck, formerly so called; all which things have been certified to me by the magistrates of the said Esopus, to have been openly bought and paid for in their presence, as appears by the return :—

Be it known to all whom it may concern, That by virtue of letters patent of his Majesty, and by the commission and authority which is given me by his Royal Highness, I have given, ratified and granted to the said Louis Du Bois and his partners,—that is, Christian Doyau, Abraham Hasbroucq, André Le Febvre, Jean Hasbroucq, Pierre Doyau, Louis Beviere, Anthoine Crespel, Abraham Du Bois, Hugue Frere, Isaac Du Bois and Simon Le Febvre, their heirs, and others having right from the said above-named persons, the said pieces of land, as well arable as [also] the forests, mountains, valleys, prairies, pasturages, marshes or ponds of water, rivers, rights of fishing, fowling, hawking and hunting; and all other profits, commodities and emoluments whatsoever, of the said piece of land and appertaining acquisitions, with their and each of their appurtenances, and all parts and parcels thereof: To have and to hold the said piece of land and acquisition, with all and singular the appurtenances and dependencies, to the said Louis Du Bois and his associates, their heirs, and others having right of property according to usage.

In consequence of the foregoing, the said Louis Du Bois and his associates, their heirs, and others having rights in perpetuity [here the connection is at fault, perhaps from an omission], and that the plantations which shall be established on the said parcels of land shall, together, be considered to be a village, and the inhabitants thereof shall have liberty to make a highway between them and the redoubt, Creek or Kill, for their convenience; and the said Louis Du Bois and his associates, their heirs, and others having right, shall render a faithful account of the survey, and make a legitimate use thereof, according to law; ren-

yielding and paying each and every year, to his Royal Highness, the rightful acknowledgment or rent of five bushels of wheat, payable at the redoubt at Esopus, to such officers as shall have power to receive it.

Given under my hand, and sealed with the seal of the province of New York the 29th day of September, in the twenty-ninth year of the reign of his Majesty, and of our Lord, 1677. [Signed],

ANDROSS.

Examined by me.

MATHIAS NICOLLS,
Secretary.

It was about this time that one of our ancestors, whose memory we honor on this occasion, came to this country. We refer, of course, to Jacques Du Bois, or as used among our Dutch friends, Jacobus, or in English, James. The year of his arrival is 1675—two hundred years ago—just the same in which Abraham Hasbrouck came. James or Jacques was a younger brother of Louis. He was apparently a man of eminent worth. He became a prominent member of the Kingston church, and equally so were his sons Jacobus and Pierre, or Peter. They married, respectively, Susanna Legg and Jeannetta Burhans, and their descendants are numerous and respectable in Ulster county. Peter early removed to Dutchess county, where his descendants have, from the first, ranked among the most useful citizens. This family bear an honored record, especially in the churches of Poughkeepsie and Fishkill. First on the list of officers and members of the ancient church of Fishkill stands the name of Peter Du Bois.

James, the emigrant, did not go with Louis to New Paltz. The most intimate relations, however, seem always to have subsisted between them and their families in those early times. These intimacies are here happily renewed after they have been measurably interrupted for nearly two hundred years.

The important enterprise of forming a colony solely for the enjoyment of religious and civil freedom, without respect to traffic, was now undertaken. The Dutch had established themselves on Manhattan Island, at Fort Orange, and at Esopus, and had brought with them the minister and the schoolmaster.

But *peltry* not *piety* best defined their motives. The Dutch enjoyed religious and civil liberty at home, and love of church and school was an element of their nature. They were Protestants. Among them the word of God was not barren. But the Huguenots fled from their native country to escape popish bigotry, tyranny and persecution, and wherever they settled their definite aim was not trade but liberty of conscience, freedom to serve God and one another. This is fully illustrated by their settlements at Oxford, near Worcester, Mass., New Rochelle, N. Y., and by this colony at New Paltz. Louis Du Bois and his associates sacrificed their prospects of worldly thrift, and entered the unbroken forests there to secure to themselves and their children a purely civil and religious asylum. *They even refused a larger grant of land at a time when all were grasping for more*, because it was unnecessary to their purpose. They were not mercenary trades-people nor socialists nor religious enthusiasts, but sensible, earnest and Godly men and women, to whom freedom in their labors and in their worship was dearer than the treasures of both the Indies.

The arrangements necessary for the departure of the colonists are complete. Business is settled, lands and houses, superfluous cattle and household goods disposed of. The designated morning of the departure arrives. I bring you to the place of assembling. Would you know the form of that ancient Kingston they are about to leave? You have but to study the present map from the junction of Greene and North Front to Main street, and you have the streets precisely as they were laid down two hundred years ago, except that Fair has been opened from Main to John. The stockade ran along the bluff at the north side of the town and followed the outer line of streets, including Main. A separate fortified place of angular form rested on Main street, having a block house at the right-angle, corner of Main and Fair streets, a bastion at the second angle, near the corner of Fair and John streets, with the hypothenuse extending so as to inclose the church lot and the log church itself, at the corner of Wall and Main streets.

It is early morning in May, 1677;—a portion of the towns-people are about to emigrate. How could the remaining citizens break the old ties! The town gathered at the place of departure. In their front was the south gate of Wall street, at their left the stockade of the separate fortified place, and on the line of it the thick walls of the church, pierced by small windows and numerous portholes for musketry.

First, I introduce to you Louis DuBois. He has been seventeen years in the country, is well known and highly esteemed. He is a large, thick-set, strong man, with Roman-French features, shrewd and active, and fitted for leadership. Now he is very animated. You see him in the quaint garb of the day. He returns your salutation affably, but in a moment is away, counselling the women in French, and the moment after leaving some direction in Dutch to an European burgher, or speaking a word with Dominie Tesschemaker, or hurrying the steps of a negro, or asking some further particulars of the country from a friendly Indian. His wife CATRINE is there also, a self-possessed woman, wisely attentive to each particular thing. Their seven children are there, and not idle; the oldest, ABRAHAM, a patentee (survivor of the twelve), now just come of age, and LOUIS, a babe. Their only daughter, SARAH, a girl of fourteen, imitates her mother's activity. She was afterward the wife of Joost Janse, and emphatically a *mother* in Israel.

I present you Christian Deyo and family.—His name, like that of Du Bois, appears on the record in various fantastic forms. Also, his brother, Pieter Deyo, a man of foresight and enterprise. He wears the belt of a soldier, clasped, as are his breeches, at the knees with buckles of polished steel. His wife deserted him and betrayed him, and remained a bigoted Catholic in France. After indescribable suffering, he joined his brother here. He returned for his property, but failed to get it. He lost his life exploring a road from New Paltz to the Hudson—the buckles were found thirty years afterward, among his bones. Salute him with respect!

I present you, also, Abraham Hasbrouck, now two years in the country. You will notice a dignity and ease in his manner only acquired by intercourse with cultivated society. His prominence here this morning is noticeable. He comes from Calais, France, and after a sojourn in the Palatinate, entered the English army, and there knew Andross, now governor of New York. The colony owes much to his influence in securing the charter. He wears side-arms; his directions are attended to.

Both Abraham Hasbrouck and his brother Jean, whom I present to you, doubtless had families.

Here is Louis Bevier. He has suffered for conscience sake, and when leaving everything of earthly value behind him in France, his own brother disowned him, and refused to bid him farewell. I present you his wife and children.

Next, Antoine Crépel, or Crispell, an intimate friend of Louis Du Bois. You notice his sailor-jacket. He formerly followed the sea, and represented the new country as a good refuge to the afflicted Huguenots, his fellow-sufferers. I present also his wife, Maddelen Joops.

Hugo Freer is an earnest and pious man, the first deacon at New Paltz.

Last, I present you Andries and Simon LeFevre. The name was eminent in the reformation of France. They had done and suffered much for religion, and their faithfulness to the cause is unchanged among their descendants to our day.

Ah! you do not know these people yet! each one has a history written in tears and blood. They are confessors for Christ, every one of them, and such as the world is not worthy of! How many are in this company? Probably about fifty, with a few domestics. We see them beside the church, in the wide street of that queer, nondescript little town, with its dilapidated palisades and gates, and its various houses in which the architecture of the Netherlands of France, of Congo, and of the Indian wigwam commingle incongruously.

Prominent in the midst of the gathering throng stand three strange looking wagons—capacious, and canvas-covered; they were well called *cars*. They are unmistakably French-built, with low wheels, deep felloes and turned spokes. They were made by French mechanics, and loaded with French goods and furniture (though, we must admit, not in such fabulous quantities as freighted the May Flower!) and there were precious little French babies stowed snugly into them. The negroes had already driven on the cattle and swine. They have said adieu; Tesschemaker has prayed;* they begin to move; the throng crowd out through the gate, as if the whole population are about to emigrate, and accompany their friends, until at length, far into the woods, the

* Thirteen years later, the Indian with his axe smote asunder the head of this good man, and left him with his dwelling to be half consumed at Schenectady.

last parting word is spoken—and the Huguenot colony of New Paltz is alone, face to face with many hardships.

Not all the Huguenot families of Kingston (the name had recently been established by Gov. Andross) left with the New Paltz colony. William E. Du Bois, our first American historian, gives a list of more than twenty French families who remained.

I cannot tell, from authentic data, the route pursued by Louis Du Bois and his fellow-colonists from Kingston to New Paltz. Intelligent persons of the neighborhood tell me that the only practicable route was the west shore of the Rondout, by way of the Green Kills, turning to the left where the road now strikes the Delaware and Hudson canal, and crossing the Rosendale at the old ford which lay at that place. Then you find a natural and comparatively easy ascent up from the valley, along the side hill, to the table lands of Rosendale, extending all the way to Springtown and New Paltz. Whatever the route may have been, the point of arrival is well known. That interesting spot was Tri-Cor, the present residence of Mr. Ira Deyo, on the west bank of the Wallkill, one mile south of the church. The name is given from the three wagons, or *cars*, used in the journey.

The opening scene in the local history of the New Paltz settlement was filled with romance and dramatic interest.

As the evening shadows were lengthening across the valley, the weary train moved slowly into an open space beside the Wallkill. Arranging the *three cars*, and making their preparations for the night as quickly as possible, they drew together to offer their thanks to God for the unfailing mercies which had brought them now at length, through perils by land and water, to their long-looked-for home. One of their number, whom we are warranted in believing to have been Louis Du Bois, reverently opened the old French Bible, and reading with suggestive emphasis the 23d Psalm, led the assembled colony in a prayer of thanksgiving and supplication. We need ask for no scene more beautiful or grand in the history of any people. Large numbers were indeed wanting, but here were all the elements of intensest interest in civil or religious history. These people were themselves the fragments of a wreck—the survivors of the lost church of France—thrown upon these shores by the angry sea. They were a few of those who remained of the defeated, scattered army of French protestants, after the long and bloody conflict had ended disastrously. Probably every family there was but a part of the old, happy household of France. Brothers, nephews, sons, had perished in dungeons, or now were mingling sighs and songs in the murderous toil of the galleys. From home and kindred and country they had fled for God and liberty. True, they were now in a perfect wilderness, and surrounded by jealous and treacherous savages. Years of toil and privation were before them—perhaps a violent death. But in their deepest hearts they felt this to be a paradise, and the mercies of God in bringing them hither like his mercies to his ancient covenant people. So praises mingled with their prayers. Thus, at length, we have arrived with our forefathers at the land of promise. God had wrought wondrously for them by His providence, and abundant blessings were yet in store for all their perils and losses.

The great mission of Louis Du Bois and his associates at New Paltz was now fairly in hand. After the merest shelter of their families, first came the equitable division of their lands, and then the definite arrangement of their civil government. The first, it would seem, was performed in a rude way; each family portion was measured off by paces, and staked at the corners. These boundaries were never changed. None were found to remove the landmarks which the fathers had set, and they remain to this day.

It was a curious custom of theirs, to apply designations to the parcels assigned to the special owners, such as these—Pashemoy, Pashecanse, Wicon, Avenyear, Lanteur, Grampase, etc. These names have survived two hundred years. The lands were at first tilled in common, and the proceeds equally divided. As their fields lay adjacent to one another, they practised a novel mode of planting so as to guard against confusion and insure concert of action in case of sudden attack by the Indians. All the field-paths and roads were made to converge to one point, which was the fortified rendezvous of the settlement. At the first alarm, every man sprang along the row in which he happened to be standing, and soon found his neighbors gathering closer to him, and in a few moments all were at the fort. This ingenious arrangement was to prevent confusion even in the densest fog.

Apropos, an amusing story is told of one Francis Rampant, an early settler. An alarm was made while the men were in the fields, and according to the rule, no man stopped to fight on his own account, but all followed the rows to the rendezvous. The number was full, with the exception of Rampant, and a party returned to bring him in. They soon found him sunk to his middle in a marshy spot, as he was heavy, and better at sinking than at running. But they found him in fair spirits; for while there, he had been attacked by a young Indian, but having seized the savage by the throat, he thrust him under the mud beside him, and, tightening his grip, he exclaimed, in a favorite phrase, "*Where were you when the king was crowned?*" The Indian was dead, and Rampant, fearing the vengeance of the tribe, returned to France. It is owing to the circumstance of his return that we have no New Paltz people of that name.

The *civil government* of the infant colony was wholly of their own devising, and differed entirely from the system in vogue at Wiltwyck and other Dutch municipalities. The twelve patentees—the "DUZINE," as they were called—were constituted the legislative and judicial body of the miniature state. The number was supplied, after the death of the original members, by annual election. Decisions in all cases referred to them seem to have been accepted as final; for though we must assume the right of appeal to the colonial government, no such appeal is known to have been made, or disputed boundary, or internal feud to have disturbed the absolute harmony of the settlement. There was no civil government other than that of the Duzine in operation at New Paltz for a period of more than one hundred years.

On March 31, 1785, the township was incorporated under the state government. The "Twelve Men" at that date, and the last in office, were Simon DuBois, Jacobus Hasbrouck, Johannes Freer, Jacob Hasbrouck, jr., Abraham Donaldson, Abraham Eltinge, Petrus Hasbrouck, Samuel Bevier, Benjamin Deyo, Isaac LeFever, Matthew LeFever and Abraham Ein. The allotments, and all decisions of the Twelve Men, were confirmed. Their "Common Book" was to be retained a reasonable time by the surveyor-general, and then deposited in the county clerk's office to be forever preserved. The records are deemed authentic evidence in court.

We come now to consider the attention paid by our forefathers at New Paltz to education and religion. We speak of education and religion, for the two were inseparably connected in their minds. An educated ministry and an intelligent people were correlative ideas. In their best days in France, the Huguenots had no less than five universities—Saumar, Montauban, Nismes, Montpelier and Sedan. As soon as the infant colony of New Paltz had secured a shelter for their families on the east bank of the Wallkill, to which they had removed, they erected a rude log building to answer the double purpose of school-house and church. It stood on the old burial-ground, beside the road yonder, where, for all these years, the precious dust of our ancestors has reposed. Here the people met for such Sabbath worship as they themselves could conduct. They drew the waters of salvation directly from the Scripture fountain, and saw the wilderness made glad and blossom as the rose. But at length, after five or six years, on January 22, 1683, a minister of their own nationality as well as faith, found his way to their secluded home. This honored man was Rev. Pierre Daillie. He came on Friday, at mid-winter, but the news spread, and on Sunday, January 24, 1683, the little church was crowded twice to hear him preach. This occasion proved one of lasting interest and blessing, and at this very moment we are sitting beneath the shadow of that fruitful vine which was planted amid the rigors of that winter's day by our ancestors. We have the original record of that day's doings, written in French by the hand of Louis Du Bois. This has been already quoted in Dr. Peltz's address of welcome.* It is the simple statement of a transaction now in the dim past, but whose blessings are as fresh as the dew which lay this morning along this valley.

Who amongst us, my friends, the descendants and kindred of Louis Du Bois, are making a record which shall be, two hundred years hence, as worthy of commemoration as this? It would seem that the church believed in the democratic method of choosing

* See page 9.

officers, but under the restriction and safeguard of qualified voters. By another authentic document we are in no doubt as to the faith or polity of the infant church. Huguenots did not use language to disguise the sense, or follow a serpentine policy to escape responsibility. The *Hasbrouck manuscript* informs us that "the inhabitants of New Paltz assembled together and formed themselves into a congregation by the name of the *Walloon Protestant Church, after the manner and discipline of the Church of Geneva.*" And afterward, when the French tongue declined and the Dutch came into use, they were still found "using and holding the discipline as at first." However, "during the life of the patentees, divine service was always held in the French language, and many years afterwards." Rev. Daillie continued pastor of the church during all the time in which Louis DuBois resided at New Paltz.

The church itself has long and honoraby loutlived its founders; a long and worthy line of pastors and elders have followed. Fifteen ministers (including three supplies) have served here. Their labors have filled this whole region with happy gospel fruits. No Romish fane desecrates this broad domain. This noble church edifice is the fifth in succession from the little log church of our fathers. The superstructure rests on a stone basement, and a number of the larger stones are from the old wall, religiously preserved because of the old initials of the founders carved upon them, as—H B for Hasbrouck, D B for DuBois, L F for LeFevre, etc. The congregations of New Hurley, Highland, Guilford, Rosendale and Dashville have gone out from the mother-church of New Paltz. While naming these churches in the immediate neighborhood, we cannot forget those in Monmouth and Salem counties, New Jersey; Bucks, in Pennsylvania; Staten Island, Poughkeepsie, Fishkill, New York, and churches in Ohio and other States. The principles upon which this church and this community were founded, being divinely appointed, were divinely blessed.

After a residence of ten years at New Paltz, Louis DuBois returned to Kingston, where many of his old French friends still lived.* He bought a "house and homelott" of DERRICK SCHOEPMES, on the north-west corner of east Front and John streets, and there spent the remaining ten years of his life.

Louis Du Bois left two wills, respecting which I quote from the "*Record*," as follows:—

"Two wills—one of which was 'the last will and testament,' and that afterwards changed by a codicil—are extant. The first is in English, the last is in Dutch; both of them, no doubt, first meditated in French. They both contain a curious provision, which may afford some insight into Louis' peculiarities of mind. In 1686, he writes: "My wife shall have the ordering of the estates; that is to say, to have the profits and perquisites of the same, so long as she remaineth a widow; but in case she cometh to remarry, then she shall have the right half of the whole estate, either land, houses or any other goods; and the other half shall be amongst the children as above-said, equally dealt," etc. In 1694, he dictates the same bequest, though in another language.

"In the usual forecast of dying husbands, we expect to read: 'In case she cometh to remarry, then she shall have her lawful dower, and no more.' It is refreshing to meet with the above act of generosity, and find it persisted in. Indeed, it amounted to a premium upon second marriage, of which, however, Catharine did not avail herself. She was also appointed executrix of the will."

This wife was that Catharine Blanshan whom he had led to the altar in the old protestant church of Manheim, on Sunday, October 10, 1655.† Well and faithfully, we may believe, did these

* All the Frenchmen of Kingston did not go to New Paltz; so that Louis had "company" in one place as well as the other. We find the following names on Kingston records, which are not on those of Paltz: Perrine, Dumont, Delamater, Lagransie, De la Montagne, Gacherie, Fanueil, Fauconnier, Bonnemere, De la Valle, Gabai, Poitiers, Saumaine, Le Maitre, Lachaire, Debuisson, Vallon, Conche, Petit Gallais, Laconte, Dupuy. It cost me some labor to hunt these out, and future inquirers may find here a clue.—[SENIOR ED.]

† It was a Huguenot custom to celebrate marriage on the Sabbath, and at the communion service. The ceremony was long, including the reading of Scripture, a lecture on the nature and duties of the marriage relation, and addresses to both bride and bridegroom, followed by the prayer and official blessing of the clergyman. At the close the groom implanted a hearty kiss upon the bride's lips, as though each would pledge the other that thereafter no word but of sympathy, kindness and love should be spoken.

venerable ancestors of ours keep the marriage vow; and amid persecutions, perils of the sea and the wilderness, among savage captors and impending death—they had been all the world to one another.

"A most interesting trait appears in the solemn introduction to his last will (says the '*Record*'), which we will give in Dutch and English:—

"'Vor eerst geef ik myn ziel aen de Almagtige Godt myn schepper, en Jesus Christus myn verlosser, en aends Hylige Geest myn hyligmaker, en myn lichaam tot de aarde van waer het saelve gecomen is,' etc.

"'For the first, I give my soul to the Almighty God my maker, and Jesus Christ my redeemer, and to the Holy Ghost my sanctifier; and my body to the earth whence it came,' etc.

"There is here no dealing in generalities, but a very explicit expression of faith in Jesus Christ and the Triune God.

"The estate was divided into eight equal parts, among the following legatees: Abraham, Jacob, David, Solomon, Louis, Matthew; children of Isaac, deceased; and children of Sarah, deceased. But in the codicil there were specific bequests altering this method, though probably preserving an equality. The farm at Hurley was divided between Jacob and Matthew.

"And now the time came that Louis DuBois must die. He had accomplished about sixty-six years upon the earth; he had lived in France, Germany and America; he had endured many sore trials and enjoyed many great blessings. He had trained up a large family, and they were well settled in life. From first to last, he had shown himself a man of singular energy of character and piety of heart and life. He was identified with almost the first settlement of this new world, and has given us an early title to the American name.

"The will of Louis having been proved on 23d June, 1696, we may conclude he died in that same month and year, and no doubt was buried in the ground of the Dutch church at Kingston."*

*It seems pretty certain that Catharine survived her husband about ten years; as in April, 1706, the heirs completed the partition of the estate, by executing certain releases according to the tenor of the codicil.

Matthias Blançon (or Blanshan, as he wrote) was no doubt her brother. He settled at Hurley, and left four daughters and a son.—[SENIOR ED.]

In concluding this sketch of Louis Du Bois, I have but little to add by way of general remark. His active life, and the valuable results which have flowed from it, must control our opinions of the man. His works do follow him. I shall here be content with quoting a few testimonials to his character. The first, by a descendant of his now among us, Mr. William E. Du Bois, has just been given. The second is from the History of the Huguenot Church of New Paltz, by Dr. Charles H. Stitt, a former pastor here. He says: "His long settlement in this country, as well as his strong mind and devoted piety, seem to have constituted him a sort of civil and religious leader in the infant colony." But with more satisfaction do I refer to the fact from which our invitation to this happy assembly sprung, that, by the free votes of those who knew him best, he was elected the first elder of this church. Men have struggled at the sacrifice of everything useful and holy to win a throne; but thus secured, I count the throne a far lower seat than the elders' bench, and descent from such a sire more honorable than the blood of perjured, persecuting kings.

The history of the New Paltz church, as well as the history of numerous other churches and communities in which the descendants of Louis Du Bois have labored, and in which the Huguenot element has been influential, proves the true vitality of protestantism, and that it is capable, not only of forming but also of maintaining, through successive generations, the best forms of civil, social and religious life. I refer with pride to the fact that the faith of our Huguenot ancestors is to-day the faith of all the churches in which their descendants have been influential. This is matter of thankfulness to God, and not of boasting in ourselves. The fact is wholly due to those divine principles which our fathers embraced at the cost of everything dear to them but life, and at life's imminent and constant hazard. I thank God that Louis Du Bois was the father of such a numerous and staunch progeny of protestants.

That persecuting church—that fell conspiracy against man's liberty and God's supreme honor—has no successful disguises against the children of those who tasted the sweets of Romanism in the loss of all their civil rights, and all their estates; in the ashes of their burnt dwellings, and in the tears and blood of their dearest kindred. Notwithstanding all her professions, while Romanism remains in America in 1875 precisely what she was in France in 1675, and boasts that she is unchanged, shall we adopt a blind charity, to our certain ruin? Rome would devour us here as voraciously as she did there, had she the power, and were it politic. You may not believe it; I pray God you, or your children, may not see the triumph of Antichrist.

I cannot close this account better than by making use of the same eloquent paragraph from Webster, which the "*Record*" appropriately quotes in the same connection: "Poetry has fancied nothing in the wanderings of heroes so distinct and characteristic. Here was man, indeed, unprotected and unprovided for, on the shore of a wide and fearful wilderness; but it was politic, intellectual and educated man. Everything was civilized but the physical world. Institutions containing, in substance, all that ages had done for human government, were established in a forest. Cultivated mind was to act upon uncultivated nature; and, more than all, a government and a country were to commence with the very first foundations laid under the divine light of the Christian religion. Happy auspices of a happy futurity! Who could wish that his country's existence had otherwise begun? who would desire to go back to the ages of fable? who would wish for an origin obscured in the darkness of antiquity? who could wish for other emblazonings of his country's heraldry, or other ornaments of her genealogy, than to be able to say that her first existence was with intelligence, her first breath the inspiration of liberty, her first principle the truth of divine religion?"

Brethren, descendants and kindred of Louis Du Bois,—REST YE IN THE FAITH OF YOUR FATHERS.

The Du Bois quartette,* from Bridgeton, New Jersey, then sang the following chant, which had been arranged for the occasion:—

I.

I am the Lord thy God, which brought thee out of the land of Egypt, and out of the house of bondage.

II.

Honor thy father and thy mother, that thy days may be long in the land which the Lord thy God giveth thee.

III.

Thou shalt dwell in the land, and thou shalt be near unto me, thou and thy children, and thy children's children.

IV.

He hath gathered us out of the land, from the east and from the west, from the north and from the south.

V.

The Lord your God hath multiplied you, and behold ye are this day as the stars of heaven for multitude.

VI.

Oh, that men would praise the Lord for his goodness, and for his wonderful works to the children of men.

VII.

Peace be within these walls, and prosperity in thy dwellings; for our brethren's sakes, we will now say, Peace be with thee. Amen.

Rev. Robert Patterson Du Bois† read the following paper on

* Robert Du Bois and Col. Edward M. Du Bois, brothers, and their two sisters. They represented the ancient settlement in southern Jersey. This effective performance was afterwards twice called for.

† Pastor of the Presbyterian church at New London, Chester county, Penna., where he has been stationed for forty years. His descent from Louis is by Jacob, Louis III., Peter, Uriah.

THE CHARACTERISTICS OF THE FAMILY.

My Friends and Kindred.

I have been invited by the executive committee to prepare a paper for this reunion of the Du Bois family and others affiliated with them. The subject of the paper has been assigned as "*The Characteristics of the Family, the Influences Producing Them, and the Influences Exerted in turn upon Society.*" I have undertaken this work with a painful sense of the difficulties in the way, arising from the great extent of the field to be surveyed, and my entire unacquaintance with the great majority of the persons about whom I am to write. Still, as it fell to my lot, about fifteen years ago, in connection with my brother William, to compile what has been called "*The Du Bois Family Book,*" and as this necessarily turns my attention somewhat to the history of the tribe, I have felt that it was my duty to respond to the request.

What is said must, of course, be very general, and large allowances must be made for exceptions to the broad statements ventured. This family have been so ramified with other names, so scattered abroad over the land, so diversified in their circumstances and surroundings, that we must expect to find with them, as with every other wide-spread race, a mingling of opposite kinds. Yet, with all this, something definite and positive may be properly said.

I.—Characteristics.

Understanding by this the general character which the branches of this family have maintained, I will speak—

1.—*As to their Intelligence.*—Those of them who came to this country, and their associates, did not come as boors and serfs, but as educated, well-informed people. Their descendants, copying after them, have been in general a reading, reflecting class, above rather than below the average in that respect in this country. They have patronized schools and colleges, book-stores, libraries and periodicals. Those who have entered the learned professions have inclined rather to the ministry, but there have been amongst them numbers of good lawyers, skilful physicians and able teachers. We have produced authors, painters and poets, and have furnished enterprising merchants and ingenious manufacturers and mechanics. We can count amongst us college professors, civil engineers, bank officers, makers of paper money and of hard money. In short, to all the varied employments of men which require thought and intelligence, we have supplied our full quota.

2.—*As to their Thrift.*—Our ancestors did not come to America as lords and gentlemen, to live upon their means, but as industrious men, to carve out their fortunes by hard work. They had to clear the forests and to improve the rude virgin soil. Hence, for the first three or four generations, they were nearly all farmers. They brought with them French taste, and Dutch neatness and industry; and so they made good farmers, and they brought up their children to the same. Very many of them have been, and many of their offspring still are agriculturists, in the old States and the new. Thus have they made the wilderness and the solitary places to be glad for them, and the desert to rejoice and blossom as the rose. Although they purchased vast tracts of land at the beginning, yet when children multiplied and these tracts were subdivided, it was found that all the sons could not have farms any longer, and so some of them had to turn to other employments. In whatever line of business they had engaged, they have been in the main thrifty and successful, with here and there exceptions. Few have been very rich; still fewer very poor. They have kept in the middle path in that respect. With all their thrift, they cannot be charged with avarice. In proof of this, we may refer to this present gathering; for we have not assembled, as many clans have done, to devise plans for securing some hoped-for legacy or to enter suit for some rich inheritance in the old mother-country, but to look each other in the face, and to extend to one another the warm grasp of brotherly affection.

3.—*As to their Social Standing.*—Intelligence and thrift almost always secure a good social status.

Hence, this family have generally met with the esteem and confidence of those whose good opinion was worth obtaining. They have been friends of good order, and so have sought and found the society of the orderly and well-behaved. They have been a marrying people, and have well obeyed the inspired law, "Be fruitful and multiply, and replenish the land." Their number indicates this; for though a census of them is out of the question, yet we know enough to state without doubt that it runs up into the thousands. It may also be said that they have not lost sight of certain other divine rules too often neglected, such as "Husbands, love your wives, and let the wife see that she reverence her husband;" and the great commandment with a promise, "Honor thy father and thy mother, that thy days may be long upon the land which the Lord thy God giveth thee." Thus we may venture to claim for our tribe a respectable and honorable standing; and a difference from many others in a readiness to cherish our traditions and genealogical records, to keep up the family tie, to recognize fortieth cousins, and to come together to celebrate our common exodus from France and Holland, our old fatherlands beyond the Atlantic.

4.—*As to their Patriotism.*—Without any reservation, they adopted this land as their own. With all its hardships, they loved it for its civil freedom and religious privileges. I never heard of one of them who left it permanently to return to the old country. When their frontier homes were assailed by savages, who carried off their wives and children, they pursued them, and by force of arms rescued the captives. When Great Britain began to oppress the colonies, they, in common with others, rose against the oppressor; and in all the dangers and conflicts of the long revolutionary struggle, bore an active and an honorable part. As a specimen of their spirit in this respect, the writer has seen a roll of a military company, formed in Pittsgrove, N. J., in 1775, containing sixty-nine names, of whom the captain, the first lieutenant, the second lieutenant and five privates were all Du Boises. In all our wars since, they have taken part; and in our late civil contest, they helped to fill up both our army and navy with officers and men. In common with all Huguenot and Dutch families, they have always been interested in national affairs, and have taken a lively part in the politics of the country.

5.—*As to Religion and Morality.*—Here too we have an honorable record. With some exceptions, as must be expected, these have ever formed striking features of the family character. In the days of the Reformation, they had conscientiously renounced popery and all its errors. Blandishments and persecutions had alike been tried to win them back, but all in vain; they never returned to it. Their protestantism led them to this wilderness, and staunch Protestants they have ever continued to be. As such, they have usually adhered to the old established evangelical creeds. Most of those who have professed faith in Christ have been found in the Dutch Reformed and Presbyterian churches. Many, especially in the line of Jacques Du Bois, have joined the Episcopalians. Some, in certain localities, have become Methodists, and a few are connected with the Baptists. It may with truth be said, that they have not been "driven about with every wind of doctrine." Christian morals have formed a component part of their religion. They have been honest, truthful, virtuous. We cannot certainly say that no rogue nor adventurer has been found amongst them, but the great mass have been upright, worthy citizens. As legislators, they have helped to make the laws; as judges, magistrates, attorneys and jurors, to administer them; but seldom, if ever, have they been found as prisoners at the bar.

II.—The Influences Producing these Characteristics.

Some of these have been already partly anticipated in what has been said. But something more may be advanced under this head.

1.—*The Persecutions that Drove them from the Old Countries.*—These have always produced a good type of Christians and of men; and these certainly helped to make our ancestors the firm, decided, principled, tyranny-hating and God-trusting people that they were, and to perpetuate these traits in their children.

2.—*Faith and Prayers of the First of the Name Coming to America.*—That they were men and women of true piety, may be seen in their coming hither under the circumstances. Here let me quote from Weiss' History of the Protestant Refugees—as has been already done by our cousin, the Rev. G. W. Du Bois, in his valuable Family Chart—the following noble declaration: "When in 1665, Louis XIV. sent to Holland and England to persuade the protestant refugees to return (under certain restrictions), many of them replied: 'We have sacrificed everything to secure peace of mind and liberty of conscience. To that end we have abandoned all that was dearest to us in life; nor will we ever again voluntarily endanger those rights and immunities so dearly purchased.'" Their faith may also be seen in the Scriptural names they gave to their children; in their so early setting up a church —that very Huguenot Reformed church and people of New Paltz who this day do honor to the memory of their fathers and ours, and give pleasure to our hearts, by extending to us so cordial and Christian an invitation to hold our reunion within their hospitable walls. Again, in their immediate calling of a pastor and maintaining of public worship; in the election of the first Louis to the office of ruling elder; in the singing of the psalm by the captive women in the speedy prospect of a cruel death; and in the religious training of their sons and daughters. Those who believe in the efficacy of faith and prayer descending to childrens' children, not only to the third and fourth, but even to the thousandth generation, will know how to appreciate this influence.

3.—*The Kind of Religion they Embraced and Practised.*—A sound evangelical creed firmly adhered to and backed up by a high-toned morality, will produce an influence for good in any community or family that can hardly be over-estimated. A system that furnished such men as Henry and John Laurens, General Francis Marion, John Jay and Elias Boudinot, sons of Huguenot sires, must tell powerfully upon all that intelligently embrace it.

4.—*The Circumstances by which they were Surrounded.*—Their simple, primitive style of living—their hard and rugged toil, earning their bread by the sweat of their brow—the entire absence of luxury and ease—the difficulties they had to encounter—were all well adapted to make them the hardy vigorous men they were, and to transmit the same iron constitution to their posterity.

5.—*The Struggle for American Independence.*—This exerted a mighty influence upon our whole nation, and, of course, upon our family, then in the fourth generation of their American life. This kindled up the patriotic fire in their breasts. This enlisted their sympathy and active co-operation in all the plans and efforts made necessary in the formation of a constitution and laws for a new representative government, established on almost entirely new principles. This helped to make them self-governing and intelligent citizens. This led to the transmission of the same character to those who have sprung from them.

III.—The Influences Exerted in turn upon Society.

"A little leaven leaveneth the whole lump." The Huguenot and Dutch elements being diffused so early as the seventeenth century through the mass of European emigrants, and thus getting the start of many others, have always been admitted by our country's historians to have brought to bear a most powerful influence for good in moulding the character of this whole American people. They greatly aided in making this a protestant nation. They helped to secure its liberty and independence. They did much to add to its enlightenment. By their industry and frugality they promoted its prosperity. What is true of the leaven of the French and Netherland refugees, is true of our family. They landed here when the colonists were few,—they intermarried with the leading families,—they multiplied rapidly. In a few generations their numbers became very great. They spread from colony to colony, and they have kept on spreading, until they are now found in perhaps every State and territory of our widely-extended Union. Eight, or even nine, generations of them have lived, or are living, in this land. Many of these have probably never known from whom they descended. But, notwithstanding, they have imbibed the spirit of their fathers, and have helped to stamp more indelibly the leading features of their character upon this republic. No mortal can tell how far this influence extends. It is too subtile for any but the Divine Mind to penetrate. The little leaven of those two noble men, Louis and Jacques Du Bois, and their noble wives, has had its influence on this mighty mass.

Thus have I hastily gone over the subject assigned. We have seen in this review that we may count among the leading characteristics of our family, intelligence, thrift, a respectable social standing, patriotism, morality and religion. We have noticed that we may ascribe this character, among other influences, to the persecutions that the first of the name had endured; to their piety and prayers; to the kind of religion they have embraced; to their early surroundings; and to the struggle for national independence. They are satisfied that they have in their turn exerted a wholesome and wide-spread power upon American society, as to numbers, freedom, liberty of conscience, education, prosperity, virtue and Christianity.

From all these things we may conclude that we have no reason to be ashamed of our lineage; that we have done well to assemble and commemorate their virtues and their deeds; that we should endeavor to hand down the memory and the practice of them to our posterity; that we should firmly resolve never to bring disgrace upon so worthy a name; that we ought to go home wiser and better men and women for this reunion; that a more intimate acquaintance with each other should hereafter be cultivated; that we should determine to rally around our country's flag and institutions, and our Saviour's cross. And may the God of our fathers and our God give us grace so to live and so to die!

The choir then sang a second anthem.

The following paper was offered by William E. Du Bois,* who was present, but unable to read it aloud. It was read by his eldest son:—

BRINGING THE TRIBE TOGETHER.

When the house is built the scaffolding is taken down, and put away.—When we have reached the place of meeting, it matters little how we came. Yet it may afford a little diversion from the weightier matters to trace the various steps by which we have been brought together this day.

Those philosophers who are limited, like the lower animals, to a single pair of eyes, and who "know nothing beyond matter and

*One of the authors of the Du Bois "Record;" Assayer of the U. S. Mint, at Philadelphia.

WILLIAM LOUIS D., who read the paper, is Treasurer and Secretary of the Philadelphia Safe Deposit and Trust Company.

motion," would quickly dispose of such an inquiry. Forsooth, it was the steamboat, the stage, the locomotive; it was the crowd of vehicles around the church; it was the independence of the pedestrian. All these, by a law of natural selection, or by a fortuitous concourse, brought us to New Paltz, instead of leaving us at home, or scattering us in all directions. This materialism—well enough as far as it goes—will do for the horses outside, to which matter and motion are all in all. But we will go a few steps beyond, and ascertain whether we had *a mind* to come, and how we got it.

Somebody must make the first motion. He may be almost nobody; it is sufficient if he can give an impulse to others, who will not leave the thing to die in his feeble hands.

Thirty years ago the writer of this narrative was taken with a strong desire to know more about his relations and ancestors. Every man is naturally entitled to two grandfathers and two grandmothers; and so there were four lines of progenitors to trace out. Without much leisure for the employment, he set to work upon it, and found the inquiry constantly growing in interest. It called for a wide correspondence extending over several years; and a few trips to New Jersey, New York State and Connecticut.

Omitting any mention of three of the lines of ancestry in which those present have no concern, and asking leave to make some use of the first person singular, I only knew, to begin with, that my father, long a Pennsylvanian. came originally from the southern section of New Jersey, and that an ancestor of his—how far back was not known—sprang from a place up the Hudson river, called Esopus.

My mother could not help me much. She replied (August, 1845), "I highly approve of your plan of the Family Record, if we can find material. But I am ashamed to say I can add very little to the stock of information. I know nothing of your father's ancestry, except that they were driven by persecution from France to Holland, in the time of Louis XIV., where they remained till their descendants lost everything of French but the name." This turned out to be about half true, and may serve to show how much dependence we may place upon tradition.

The first thing to do was to explore Pittsgrove township, and the neighboring towns of Bridgeton and Salem, in southern Jersey. There we (my brothers with me) made new acquaintances, visited old homesteads, explored family Bibles, hunted for ancient documents. Herein we were greatly aided by an intelligent, excellent man, Moses Richman, Esq., husband of one of our cousins, and now deceased. In particular, an old knapsack, which was lying in a garret, turned out a treasure of old deeds; family letters from cousins at Hurley and thereabouts to cousins in the Jersey settlement; subscription papers—very much duboised—for building a church in Pittsgrove; and a military roll, commanded and partly manned by Du Boises, for the revolutionary war. [The roll was here shown. The captain, Jacob D., born in 1719, was a great-grandson of the first Louis.]

One of the most interesting discoveries was the old homestead of the third Louis, built soon after his removal from Esopus to Pittsgrove. It was then standing, and inhabited; but with the usual regard for antiques, has been taken down. It dated back to about 1725. I stood in front of this house with a reverential awe. No doubt it represented the usual style of farm-houses in those days—good enough for the owner of a thousand acres. A sketch of it was made at the time by my brother Samuel—accustomed to the brush and pencil.

There were two front doors, one of them the great inlet, the other evidently not much used. The former introduced you at once to the large room, with its huge fire-place, its immense joists or timbers, strong enough for a cathedral, and its few and small windows. This was the general rendezvous of the family and visitors, and served for kitchen, dining-room and sitting-room. Alongside was the lesser room, better furnished, and used only on great occasions. The exterior was shingled all over, sides and roof. There was but one main floor or story, with a half-story or sleeping loft above. The panes of glass in the windows were very small. One of them is here shown; it measures 5½ by 3½ inches, clear of the putty,—hardly large enough for one to look through with both eyes.

But while there was such simplicity in the old style of living, their manner of address, at least in writing letters, was formal and stately. More than a century ago, when a young man of genteel training would write to his mother, instead of beginning with "Dear Mother," he would say "Honored Madam." Something like this we found in the old knapsack; in particular, a letter of Miss Gerritje Bogardus, of Kingston, to Jacob Du Bois, of Salem. She addressed him as "My Honored Cousin." This was an early honor, for Jacob was only twenty-four years old. This letter is dated in 1743, and is in Low-dutch.

Another letter (obtained elsewhere) dated in 1752, from Rachel Du Bois, living at the Perkiomen settlement, Montgomery county, Pennsylvania, to her grandfather, Solomon Du Bois, shows this deference in a marked degree, as well as much cultivation of mind and heart. A short extract is worth listening to. She says: "Honored and Much-beloved Grandfather: Respect for you was in my mind from my youth. But I have had neither time nor opportunity to evince it. The young should continually hold the aged in honor and esteem. Therefore I desired it; and to that end was my prayer to God. It would afford me great joy to hear from you; in short, I have often wished to enjoy your agreeable presence and to see your face, but have not as yet been so fortunate. Though we cannot see each other on earth, yet I know we shall in Heaven."

She then informs him that, with the approbation of her father, she is shortly to be married.

Rachel had three sisters, but no brothers; and our name is extinct in that settlement. It may be said, incidentally, it does not follow that a Du Bois may settle in a fertile place, and perpetuate his name by hundreds.

This letter was also written in Low-dutch, and a copy of it, with a translation, was furnished me nearly thirty years ago.

This term, "Low-dutch," is apt to create a wrong impression; as if the people, or their language, were of an inferior sort. It refers entirely to the geographical position of the Netherlands, lower down and nearer the sea than the German highlands. As for the language, it seems a pleasant half-way between German and English; and as for the people, there is none upon earth which occupies a nobler position in history. For industry, thriftiness, neatness, intelligence, bravery and independence, they have ever stood in the front rank; and we may well be proud of the Dutch blood in our veins.

But now we come to the discovery of the "missing link;" and it came in good time.

It was late in the autumn of 1845 that I happened (a rare thing) to look over the printed list of arrivals at our hotels, in Philadelphia; and there saw, "Gilbert Du Bois and wife, Ulster county, N. Y." Instantly it occurred to me that here might be an opening to the hidden mystery of my Huguenot ancestry. I failed to meet with him, as he was in a hurry to be off and finish up the wedding trip; but my note to him on that occasion led to a correspondence which gradually unraveled the whole story, so far as our American ancestry goes; and the interchange of letters being kept up to this day, has cemented a friendship and fellowship beyond all price.

I need not here tell with what interest and assiduity he pursued this inquiry, although pressed with the cares of an important public office, and afterwards with the oversight of a manufactory, and other active business.

*In the summer of 1846, three of us (Charles, William and Louis) resolved upon an exploring expedition, to see what kind of a place and people they were, and whether they would recognize cousins at least ten degrees removed. We went up the river to Poughkeepsie, the nearest point to the Paltz valley. But we found no public conveyance to New Paltz. The only way of access was to procure a horse and vehicle at the ferry, and find our way over the hills. From the west of the highlands, looking down and along the Wallkill valley, we saw a charming landscape of fields and woods and farm-houses, hemmed in, and yet with abundant room, between mountainous ridges. It seemed as if the people had found that long-sought and sighed-for retreat, where

"Far from the madding crowd's ignoble strife,
Their sober wishes never learned to stray;
Along the cool sequestered vale of life,
They kept the noiseless tenor of their way."

*The account of these visits was not read at the meeting.

We reached the village, a neat town of some fifty houses, and betraying no signs of antiquity, except an old grave-yard.* We halted at a sort of an inn, whose appointments showed that the arrival of a stranger was unusual, and almost unwelcome. There was a place to drink (sober drink only, I am pleased to say), but scarcely a place to eat or sleep.

But as soon as we got into the hands of Gilbert Du Bois and his brother-in-law, Dr. Reeve, men whom we never saw before, we were, as the common saying is, "all right." They welcomed us, and made much of us; entertained us in their houses; took us about in their carriages; described everything. We were entirely at home; and more need not be said.

The next season (1847), two of us (William and Louis) were there again, approaching by the way of Kingston. It was needful to go there, to continue the examinations of church and office records, which Gilbert had begun.

The dominie, Mr. Hoes, received me courteously, and yet with an air of suspicion. "A good many people," he said, "had been there lately, to search the old church book. They wanted to prove themselves heirs of Anneke Janks [or Jansz], and to have part in the proceeds of a law suit"—which was then the talk of Kingston and New York, and almost everywhere.†

* The grave-yard of the old church was densely crowded with tombstones, most of them of a perishable kind of sand-stone, whose inscriptions were not easily deciphered. The oldest name we saw was Hasbrouck, 1723. The oldest of our name was Abraham Du Bois, whose epitaph appeared as follows:—

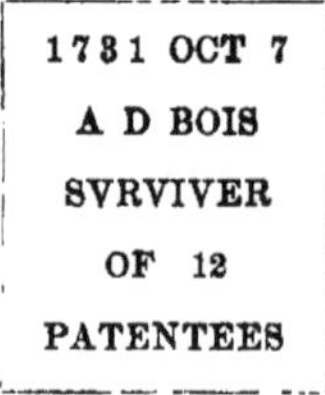

1781 OCT 7
A D BOIS
SVRVIVER
OF 12
PATENTEES

This was the eldest son of the original Louis, and a Frenchman born. And we have here the interesting fact, that he was the last of the original proprietors of the New Paltz tract.

† Few things gave me more pleasure than to meet again with Rev. Dr. J. C. F. Hoes, at the Kingston church, after twenty-eight years. He has now no pastoral charge, but continues to preach occasionally.—[SENIOR ED.]

I soon made him understand that my errand was of a very different sort. It was to find—I hardly knew what; something about Du Bois. And you may imagine with what feelings I stumbled upon the following entry, almost at the beginning of the book:—

"Oct. 9, 1661.
Vadde van dit kint Loui Duboi.
Modder Cattery Blancsan.
Kint Jacob.
Getruygen Antoy Crepel, Maddeleen Joonse."

In plain English, somewhat paraphrased,—On the 9th October, 1661, there was presented for baptism, by the father, Louis Dubois, and the mother, Catharine Blançon, a child named Jacob, being only a few days old. The witnesses or sponsors (then usual in the Dutch church) were Anthony Crispel and Magdalen Janse.

Here, then, I found "Moses in the bulrushes;" the baby Jacob, so named as a sequence to Abraham and Isaac, or else after his uncle Jacques, not yet come over. Here was the first American Du Bois; my own ancestor.

Thanks to you for this old book, good dominies Blom and Hoes, two centuries apart. Thank you, Louis and Catharine, for your pious act, and putting yourselves and your child on the record. Thank you, attentive sponsors, for seeing it through.

(We excuse the spelling. Orthography is, at any rate, a modern nicety).

And you, a numerous seed, who trace your lineage to this little Jacob, consider in what peril you stood of your very existence, when it was only by the sweet and plaintive song of his mother that the murderous purpose of the savage Indians was delayed until Louis and his party came up and rescued wife and child from a cruel death.

Thus has it happened, times innumerable, that the smallest circumstance has produced the greatest and most lasting effects. Thus the little Moses was preserved by the mere chance of Pharaoh's daughter going to the Nile at the critical moment; with what vast results from that day till now, and forever! "This is the Lord's doing, and it is marvellous in our eyes."

In the same book, Isaac was recorded as having been "geboren tot Manheym in de Palsz." This showed where Louis had taken refuge in the old country; not in Holland, but in Germany.

But it is needless to continue the details of discoveries made by Gilbert and myself, with numerous helps here and there. Nor need I dwell upon the pleasure of finding the first records of the French church at Paltz, and rendering them into English.

How pleasant it was to complete the connection—to know that Louis begat Abraham, Isaac and Jacob, with other patriarchs and mothers in Israel, too numerous here to mention; that Jacob begat Louis; and Louis, Peter; and so on, down, down, making the eighth American generation in our little boys and girls. We are Americans of long standing and prior right; in fact, we belong to the aboriginals; not the red, but the white.

The Family Record was printed in 1860. No doubt it helped to stir up others—especially on the Dutchess side of the river—not only to ascertain the connection of the two branches, Louis and Jacques, but also to get beyond the American beginning, and see how far backward we could trace the family in Europe. There was *one* brotherhood, which had special facilities and capabilities for prosecuting this difficult task; and we shall all feel a lasting obligation to them. What they have accomplished, you have been informed. The Hudson river draws no dividing or dubious line between us. And if, across the great water, we cannot reach back to Peter Du Bois of Ghent, we have still made a considerable ascent. Various circumstances, already stated, seem to indicate an armorial ancestry. But we would rather derive our nobility from those who braved every danger and suffered every loss to maintain a holy faith and a pure conscience.

Here allow me reverently to borrow the language of St. Paul, and say to all this clan,—If we are mindful of that country from which we came out, no doubt we have opportunity to return. It is true, France is considerably smaller than Texas, and has a population nearly as great as all the United States, and must therefore be full enough; but they make Americans welcome, especially if they have money to disburse. We shall find them courteous, agreeable, gay, and excitable, beyond all people;—in science, and some of the arts, in advance of us; in agriculture;

and enterprise generally, behind us; and in respect to morality, social order and home comforts, just what Jesuitism and Nothingism are sure to produce. It is a land alternately dominated by Bourbons and Bonapartes, by red republicans and Romish priests. It is a people ready to rush into a war for glory, and sometimes coming out without any—as in the instances of Russia, Mexico and Germany. They drove us out; we are content to stay out. We desire a better country; and here we have it. If it is not all we could wish, we must help to make it better. And let us remember that we are here only passengers and pilgrims. The next centenary, if one should be celebrated, will find none of us here.

How interesting it would be if we could exhibit veritable portraits of Louis and Jacques, and their wives. Photography came too late; but painting was in all its glory when they left. And if they could have imagined that such a scene as this was to be enacted, they surely would have sat to Rembrandt for their pictures, and brought them along to let us see their faces. Did they look Frenchy? No doubt. Were they good-looking? We will take that for granted. Would the fashion of their coats and bonnets suit us? Probably not.

Will some keen artistic eye please to run over this assembly, and see if there are lineaments that link us together? How far can a family resemblance be carried? We sometimes say of a boy, he favors his grandfather, by a pretty hard strain of the imagination. But whether all of us together could furnish a fancy sketch of our first fathers, any one who looks around will be apt to doubt.

In this small pile of "bric-a-brac," now nearly through with, it was my purpose to show the various steps by which we have been brought together. And truly it was necessary that some man, or set of men, of vigorous purpose, should conceive the idea, and resolve to carry it out. Few persons can imagine how much energy and perseverance it requires to do such a thing. At the first mention, some will approve; some will doubt; and some will give a dash of cold water. We needed, therefore, such an executive committee, collected from localities wide apart. And above all, we must have an *Anson DuBois*, qualified, like the renowned Admiral Anson, to encounter and overcome all difficulties. He must endure this little bit of praise, for we are greatly indebted to his successful command.

In fine, we are brought together by the cordial invitation of the Huguenot Reformed church and people of New Paltz. They are the right people, in the right place; and for the time, so are we. Here Louis and Catharine walked together to church, and sang the old French psalms. And if the church has been renewed, it is because Paltz ever keeps New. But we look up to the same Paltz Rock that was in the gaze of our ancestry, and we admire the same Wallkill which enlivens and fertilizes this pleasant valley. May the two be a type of our unison and fellow-feeling, "yesterday and to-day and forever."

On re-assembling the next morning (Thursday), the meeting was opened by prayer from Rev. Benjamin Du Bois Wyckoff,* of Freehold, N. J.

The president announced the programme for the day.—A poem written for the occasion; addresses by representatives of kindred families; letters of fellowship from relatives unable to be present; and finally, after a second noon-day repast, as before, a visit to the First Reformed Church at Kingston, in acceptance of a cordial invitation from the consistory, at which place the reunion would terminate.

The following poem† was read by Patterson Du Bois, of Philadelphia:—

OUR NEW PALTZ.

I.

PRELUDE.

From the old mansion window, reviewing the scene
  Made sacred in childhood to frolic and game,
Old Memory asks if the long years between
  Forbid that herself and the child be the same;

* A descendant of Dominie Benjamin Du Bois, of Monmouth. Dr. Wyckoff was a missionary to northern India for fifteen years.

† Afterwards published in the Hudson "Star." The writer has been, for the past nine years, one of the assistants in the assaying department of the U. S. Mint.

So I know of a balcony built 'neath the sky,
  Whence I turn and look back on the broad earth below;
And I wonder if this was *my* home, and if I
  Am the life that it knew in the long years ago.

Had I brothers and sisters?—I call them kin now—
  And the shoot now the shade of a mighty tree weaves:—
There's a sway in the branch, there's a rock on the bough,
  And a sweet breath from Heaven is rustling the leaves.
'Tis the spirit of brotherly-love, and it comes
  With a voice that is echoed from far-distant days;
And pleads in the name of our freedom, our homes,
  Reunion in gratitude, gladness and praise!

II.

Our fathers' home!—Thou lovely vale,
  Ye mountains decked with farm and wood;
Your memories to us entail
  A legacy of brotherhood.

Dear be to us this sacred ground,
  Here fondly let our spirits roam—
Where first a life within us found,
  A peaceful Refuge, Rest and Home.

Home makes a tie none can forget,
  And thence our best emotions start;
One pulse is beating in us yet,
  On earth the veins, in Heaven the heart.

Such life must have its single soul
  To strike the many-noted chord;
And every portion claim the whole
  To swell its anthem to the Lord.

Then join your hearts, that from this hour
  Ye stand a firm and God-linked chain,
To bind that God-forsaken power
  That craved your blood and loves the stain!

Your stories are my stories, told
  In ever varied tongue and tone;
And, as in leaves, how manifold
  The differences that make us one!

A thousand differences of kind,
  Aye! and a thousand of degree;
But in each fruit one seed I find
  That hath true counterpart in me.

Though strangers still, though each life seems
  A hidden maze of trait and lot,
One polar star in each soul gleams
  That draws me to its vital spot.

And there with joyous steps I steal,
  And hear a voice from other days
That sings of rest, and makes me feel
  There is a prophecy in praise.

Our fathers' praises we renew,
  For hither all our hearts have come
To prove the Truth our fathers knew,
  Itself is Refuge, Rest and Home.

III.

O temple of our ancestors,—
  Whose incense, breathed from cliff and sod,
Gave life for death, and peace for wars,
  And knew no priest but Christ in God.

No altar smoke here lifted toward
  A costly ceil and dusky dome,
That shuts the creature from his Lord,
  And binds his worship down to Rome.

Our fathers reared no pictured wall,
  No Virgin's shrine, no idol fane;—
No prison-like confessional,
  Where priests turn parish guilt to gain.

Not here could weak and wanton man
  Assume divine vicegerency—
Profess the gospel as his plan,
  Yet fear to make its pages free.

No foothold here for mockeries—
  For soulless forms no livelihood—
Whose swelling growth is of disease,
  And ignorance is staple food.

Then who are they whose voices swell
  This mighty dome with new-born hopes?
A God-directed Israel,
  Freed from the tyranny of popes!

The voices from the waves that fret
  The noble Hudson's peaceful shore,
Seem mocking now the cruel threat
  Once echoed from the galley oar.

Did savage menace? 'Twas release!
  The whoop was better than the mass;
The howling wilderness was peace,
  And papal threats but tinkling brass.

Then any hands that lifted be,
  By far had better strike than mock;
For noble souls would sooner flee
  The crozier than the tomahawk!

Not fugitives from justice then,
  Not bands to plunder and maraud,
But heretics to cruel men,
  Whose creed was heresy to God,—

Who dared to place their church before
  The Head they claimed for it above,
Pretending, by a cruel war,
  To gain the hearts He seeks for love.

Not hopes of conquest or of gain
  Behind our fathers' motives stood—
Like wild adventurers from Spain,
  Who left no influence for good.

And prince or peasant, be they what,
  We rate them not by earthly things;
The spirit of the HUGUENOT,
  Was nobler than the blood of kings.

For royal blood is hot with strife,
  And every vein with death is stored,
But Truth grows mightier as its life
  Streams by the adversary's sword!

Drunk with the blood of noble lives
  Were all the Babylonish crew;
But, ah! the living gospel thrives
  On deeds like St. Bartholomew!

And what are painted shield and crest
  And all the show that power weaves,
When kings bow down, by popes oppressed,
  And armies shake like aspen leaves?

Not much I ween; their memories rot—
  While all the world with fervor starts
To laud the fearless HUGUENOT,
  Whose shield is blazoned on our hearts!

The Truth they knew, the Faith they loved,
  Were shield and crest and coronet;
Their principles, by God approved,
  Support and bind this nation yet.

Then, who shall say our Faith is blind,
  Or deem its sight a fantasy?
No other motive of the mind
  Dares make its record half so free!

No other motive of the heart
  Is half so sweet or half so strong;
No other plays a nobler part,
  Performs so much, endures so long!

IV.

L'ENVOI.

Now, Brothers by blood,—more, Brethren by Faith,
There's a thought that is borne to us all ere we part:—
The life in us now is a rescue from death,
And its trials have brought us a peace for the heart.

Though silently on, by his monarchy draped,
To our free land the tyrant is crossing the flood—
His spirit the same that our fathers escaped,
His garments still dyed with the redness of blood,
Oh, say! shall he whirl *us* about on his breath—
Prepare for our children the fagot and stake,
When our very existence here proves that the faith
Of our fathers hath peace which no power can break?

Nay—*the answer is ours!* and we dare not rely
On the merits of those who have left us their name,
But girding their armor, 'tis ours to defy
The power whose record is covered with shame!
Then stand to the world, not in pride or self-laud,
But praying that History lift off the veil
From the future of all, who will trust in our God
Redeeming the promise that *Truth shall prevail!*

Addresses were made by representatives of collateral branches—

EDMUND ELTINGE, Esq., of New Paltz.

Rev. HASBROUCK DU BOIS, of New York city.

Rev. Dr. C. E. CRISPELL, Professor in the Theological Seminary, Holland, Michigan.

Rev. PAUL T. DEYO, of Greene county, N. Y.

LOUIS BEVIER, Esq., of Ulster county, N. Y.

Rev. JAMES LE FEVRE, of Middlebush, N. J.

ALEX. MCKIM DU BOIS, of Carlinsville, Illinois, was called upon, but did not feel prepared to take part.

The President produced a bundle of congratulatory letters—from J. DILL DU BOIS (son of Gilbert D.), residing at Portland, Oregon; Rev. Prof. CHARLES SCOTT, D. D., of Holland, Michigan (who has long taken an active interest in bringing to light the old local history); Rev. ABRAM CANTINE DU BOIS, of Auburn, Placer county, California; Judge T. R. WESTBROOK, at Saratoga; Prof. WILLIAM H. BREWER, of Yale College; Dr. HENRY A. DU BOIS, of New Haven; Rev. CHARLES W. BAIRD, of Rye, N. Y.; Dr. ABRAM DU BOIS, of New York city; Dr. FRANK L. DU BOIS, Surgeon U. S. N., on board the steamship Michigan, cruising in Lake Superior; A. SCHOONMAKER, Esq., attorney-at-law, Kingston; Gen. GEORGE H. SHARPE, New York city; F. E. WESTBROOK, Esq., New York; Lieut. ALEX. DU BOIS SCHENCK, U. S. Artillery (dated from University of Iowa): Hon. A. BRUYN HASBROUCK, St. Remy, near Kingston; WILLIAM H. DU BOIS, Esq., Hensonville, Greene county, N. Y.; Prof. ISAAC E. HASBROUCK, Rutgers College; Rev. Dr. S. M. ANDREWS, Doylestown, Pa., and Mrs. LEAH L. DALE, of Paradise, Lancaster county, Pa.

There was also a letter from Hon. JESSE K. DUBOIS, of Springfield, Illinois, in reply to an invitation (as the others were), in which he states that he has no connection whatever with our stock, his father having been an emigrant from Canada, and a Catholic; but he is himself a Presbyterian. The letter was cordial in its expressions.*

Rev. R. P. Du Bois proposed the following vote of thanks, which was heartily adopted:—

The descendants of Louis and Jacques Du Bois, so happily assembled in a family reunion at New Paltz. do hereby return their heartfelt thanks to the pastor, elders and deacons of this ancient church, for their kind invitation to us to observe our celebration in their house of worship. We would also express our gratitude to the families of the congregation for so hospitably entertaining us at their homes; to the choir of the church and the Du Bois Quartette from Bridgeton, N. J., for the delightful music they have afforded us, and to the friends of our own and other names who have presented to us the papers and letters and addresses to which we have listened with so much interest and pleasure. We trust we shall never forget our delightful visit to this place and people, and hope they will never have reason to regret their brotherly invitation.

On motion, W. E. Du Bois was requested to assist in preparing the proceedings for publication.

The President suggested the insertion of pictures of relics, old houses, and deceased persons of prominence bearing the family name.

* Dubois county, Indiana, took its name from the father of this gentleman.

For the rest, we quote the well-expressed report of the *Kingston Freeman*:—

"Rev. Dr. Peltz, in a few well-chosen remarks, thanked the audience for their attendance and interest. He eulogized the character of the gathering, and spoke in terms of high praise of the subject-matter of essays and papers read. He spoke very feelingly of the fraternal nature of the gathering, and bade farewell to the departing guests in a courteous, kind and impressive manner.

"After a vote of thanks to the President, for the able manner in which he had discharged his office, and the singing of the Doxology, the meeting adjourned.

"Refreshments were served in the basement, which were partaken of by the company, and after singing 'Auld Lang Syne,' they proceeded to the railway station and embarked for Kingston.

THE VISIT TO KINGSTON.

"The train arrived at two o'clock, and the party proceeded to the First Reformed Church.

"Rev. Anson Du Bois spoke a few words by way of introducing the party, and Rev. D. N. Vanderveer followed with an address of welcome in his eloquent and graceful style, in conclusion congratulating the company on the object of the reunion and the success that had attended it, and giving them a cordial welcome to the church with which their ancestors were so closely connected.

"To this address Rev. Anson Du Bois replied in a happy vein, and concluded by calling on the Du Bois Quartette to favor the company with some music, to which they responded.

"After this the company spent the time in an informal exchange of familiarities, examining the old Dutch records of the church, wandering about the old churchyard, &c., until they finally separated." *

And thus we honored our fathers and mothers. We called to mind the days of old, and we kept such a Passover as there had not been since the days of our fathers.

* Hon. A. Bruyn Hasbrouck was expected to take part in these exercises, but, to our great regret, was unavoidably prevented.

NOTES AND ADDITIONS.

I.—Children of Louis.

We are requested to insert this chapter from the *Record*, printed in 1860. It gives a starting-point, from which each branch can make its own connection, and continue its own history. (Some alterations have been found necessary.)

"It would be curious to inquire what is the combination of circumstances which makes a man the patriarch of his tribe—which causes him to be pointed out, by common consent, as the founder of this or that family connection. We do not at all intend to take up room with a discussion of that subject; but will only remark, that any man who has earned that distinction must not expect that all or, indeed, any one of his half-dozen or dozen children shall stand out upon the genealogical chart as prominently as himself. He has done so much for them, it may be, as to leave little room for that bold and hardy exertion which is requisite to make a conspicuous character. They may naturally be as bright and capable as their sire, but they lack the opportunity.

"All that we have to say of the many children of Louis will take less space than has been given to Louis himself. This, it is true, is not for want of will, but of materials. We have already set down their names in order, and given the dates of births, so far as ascertained.

"I. Abraham was born at Mannheim, in Germany. He was one of the twelve patentees of New Paltz, and the last survivor of them. He died October 7th, 1731, aged about 74 years. His wife was Margaret Deyo. Their children, by the record, were—Abraham, baptized in 1685; Leah, in 1687, who married Roeliff Elting; Rachel, 1689; Catharine, 1693. We have from other sources the names of Benjamin, Margaret and Mary. To this last daughter—who had married Philip Ferrie (now spelt Verree), a native of Lindau, near the Rhine—he gave a thousand acres of land, which he had patented, in 1717, in the Pequea Settlement, in Lancaster county, Pennsylvania. To this tract they removed, where they had eight children, from whom are many descendants. Other Du Boises went also from Esopus to Lancaster county.

"II. ISAAC was also a German born. He was married at Kingston, in 1683, to Marie Hasbrouck; was one of the patentees of New Paltz, and died there June 28th, 1690, aged about 31 years. Their children were Daniel, born 1684, married Mary Lefevre; Benjamin, 1687; Philip, 1690.

"III. JACOB was the first American of our line; born at Kingston, October, 1661. He settled upon a farm of his father's at Hurley, and married into a Dutch family. His wife's name was Gerritje Gerritsen; she was the daughter of Gerrit Cornelissen, who was the son of Cornelius Van Nieuwkirk. The reader will perceive here the ancient custom of taking the parent's first name as a surname for the offspring, a practice which accounts for a great many surnames in every country. Cornelius Van Nieuwkirk, who must have been a native of Holland, was probably born about the year 1600.

"Their children were no less than eleven in number—Magdalena, Barent, Louis, Gerritje, Sarah, Isaac, Gerrit, Catharine, Rebecca, Neeltje and Johannas. Four of the daughters died young, or unmarried. Of Barent and Louis, emigrants to New Jersey, we shall speak particularly in the coming chapter. Sarah, born about 1700, was married to Conrad Elmendorf; their descendants are living at Hurley. Isaac, born 1702, had one son. Gerrit, born 1704, went with his brothers to Jersey, but returned to Hurley after his father's death. He had three children—Gerritje, Conrad and Tobias. Each of these sons had nine children. The family of Conrad has spread into Ohio, Michigan and Missouri. The children of Tobias were scattered in various counties of New York. We return to Catharine, who was married to Petrus Smedes. Lastly, Johannes, or John, had seven children—Jacob, Cornelius, Petrus, Abraham, John, and two daughters. Jacob, the ancestor of all these, died about June, 1745, in his 84th year.

"IV. SARA, married to Joost Jansen.

"V. DAVID married Cornelia Varnoye, 1689. He was living in 1731. Their descendants are in Rochester, Ulster county.

"VI. SOLOMON naturally comes next to David. About 1692, at the age of 23, he married Trintje Gerritsen, sister of Jacob's wife. Their children were therefore 'double cousins.' Solomon settled on part of the land owned by his father at New Paltz, though not within the patent. During a long life of industry and good management he accumulated much landed property, not only in that region, but also in Greene county, and in Pennsylvania, at a place called Pockioma, which we conjecture was the same as Perkiomen, in Montgomery county. In his last will, a single tract in the Wallkill valley, containing three thousand acres, was given to one of his sons (Cornelius), subject to certain payments; and from the whole tenor of the will, it is inferred that the value of this tract was about one-sixth of his entire estate.

"He was a prominent member and officer in the French church—which eventually became the Dutch church—of New Paltz; and being elected to civil trusts for many years, evidently enjoyed the confidence of his fellow-citizens. He died in February, 1759, in the 90th year of his age.

"He had eight children—1. Jacomyntie (Jemima, in English, and pronounced Yah-co-mine-chee, a name repeatedly occurring in the family connection), born in 1693, was the one referred to above as having married her double cousin. This was Barent, the oldest son of Jacob Du Bois, of whom and of their descendants we shall speak in the next chapter. They were married in 1715, and had eight children. 2. Isaac, who settled at Pockioma, in Pennsylvania (probably Perkiomen), where his father had bought lands. He had four daughters. 3. Benjamin, who settled at Cattskill, N. Y. 4. Sarah, who married Simon Van Wagenen, of New Paltz. 5. Helena, or Magdelena, who married Josiah Elting, of New Paltz. 6. Catharine, intermarried with Peter Low, of the same place. 7. Cornelius, whom and his children we shall introduce again in the next chapter. 8. Hendricus (or Henry), who married Jannitje Hoogteyling, of Kingston.

"VII. REBECCA, born in 1671.

"VIII. RACHEL, born in 1675. These died in early life.

"IX. LOUIS, born about 1677, was married to Rachel Hasbrouck in 1601. To this stock the families of Broome and Tioga counties, N. Y., of Lycoming county, Pa., and others, belong; also, Wm. M. Du Bois, of Elmira, N. Y.

"X. MATTHEW was the last child of the first Louis. It appears that, having exhausted the line of names of the Old Testament patriarchs, and then interpolated one for himself, he was beginning again with the New Testament evangelists; but his plan was cut off, for Mark, Luke and John never saw the light. Matthew was born about 1679, and was married to Sarah Mattheysen. They had at least one son, and his name was Louis. Matthew inherited half of the Hurley farm, and also his father's house and lot in Kingston, where he resided, at least in 1706. With him closes the history of Louis' children.

"Having thus disposed of this generation, we must say something of the times in which they lived, so far as can be gleaned from the old records.

"The rude account of a tax which was laid by the provincial government shows the simplicity of the style of living, and how little it takes to make us comfortable when we have known nothing better. Each chimney and each stove was assessed. Solomon gloried in two chimneys and two stoves, but in the houses of Jacob and David we find one spacious hearth and stove serving for all the cooking and the warming of the entire family, for the man-servant and maid-servant, and any stranger who might be within the gates.

"The hunting of wolves was a manly diversion and a public benefit; the receiving a legal bounty upon their scalps was an incidental gain. In this doubly good work our ancestors figured as well as their neighbors, and the old records disclose how much they made by it.

"In 1718 the number of taxables in Paltz was twenty-eight, of whom all were French but five. But in a militia muster-roll of 1738, of the same town, only thirty names are French, out of ninety-four. The French language was still in use in 1712, as appears by a legal writing of that date; but it was dying out for want of schoolmasters, and, from the incursions of the Dutch, in the way of intermarriage.

"In twenty-two years after the death of the first Du Bois, we find that in Ulster county his descendants were as one to forty-six in the whole number of taxables, and as one to twenty-one in the amount of property. About one-third of the value of taxable property in New Paltz was in the name of Du Bois. Abraham was rated at £310; Jacob (at Hurley), £290; Matthew (at Kingston), £195. To form a proper idea of these sums at that time, let it be observed that the price of 'a stone house, barn and lot,' in Kingston, was £88 in 1731."

II.—Descendants of Jacques.

A large chart, with the above title, has recently been printed and distributed. The compiler, Rev. George W. Du Bois, makes this note upon it: "Except in certain lines of descent, this chart is incomplete, for the reason that I have not been able to obtain full family registers in every case." And yet the wonder is that it is so complete. It gives the result of more labor than is often expended upon a pretentious volume.

Of course, it is superfluous for us to do more than refer to these tables. Every living Du Bois, of that side of the house, can, with this help, trace his line back to the family in Artois. And we need not insert here any details of the patriarch Pierre, or Peter, son of Jacques, as they will be found in a succeeding paper.

The "lives and fortunes" of Louis and Jacques were very diverse, in two particulars. They both came to the wilds of America to live and die; but Louis lived here thirty-six years, and Jacques hardly more than one year. Louis left seven sons to keep up the name; Jacques left three—perhaps not more than two who were married. As a consequence, the descendants of the one considerably outnumber those of the other in our day. By a list obtained in 1858, the number of taxables surnamed Du Bois, in Ulster only, was one hundred and forty.* Judging from the Jacques chart, and from what we learn from Dr. John C. Du Bois, of Hudson, the taxables on that side, wherever they live, do not *now* exceed one hundred; perhaps not over eighty. And then, taking the country over, from Rhode Island to Oregon, we might put the tax-list of Louis' side at full three hundred.

* "We have here, about three miles south of the village of New Paltz, on both sides of the Wallkill, over a dozen Du Boises, all farmers, tilling the same land that Louis and his sons were first settled on, and which has never been out of the name."—*Letter of Jacob G. D.* This gentleman, a descendant of Solomon, shows an unbroken record of his line. Some are settled in Ohio.

It is considered fair to multiply taxpayers by five to arrive at the whole census of men, women and children called by this name and of this stock. At this moment they would doubtless amount to two thousand.

There must be as large a number, equally partakers of the blood, whose maternal ancestors surrendered the name by marriage.

And yet the name is not common, except in a few localities. Had it been some other that we might mention, it would have been difficult to disentangle. As it is, we all seem to know instinctively whether we sprang from Catholic Dubois, kinsmen of the Cardinal, or whether from Huguenot Du Bois, hailing from Artois and from Kingston.—[SENIOR ED.]

III.—THE HUGUENOT MEDALS.

We have thought that the history of a Huguenot colony, as this is in some sort, would be properly illustrated by a fac-simile of these famous monuments of barbarity. Although often spoken of, they are rarely to be seen.*

No. 1. Medal struck in Rome in honor of the massacre of St. Bartholomew's eve.

Head of the Pope. Legend, GREGORIVS XIII. PONT. MAX. AN. I.; i. e., *Gregory XIII. Chief Pontiff, year* 1. Reverse, the Angel of Death, with sword and cross, pursuing and killing. Legend, VGONOTTORVM STRAGES, 1572; i. e., *Slaughter of the Huguenots.* This medal is in the highest style of art.

The Papal engraver, in Latinizing *Huguenot*, used his own spelling; but *Vgonot* means the same.

No. 2. Medal struck in Paris on the same occasion.

Head of the King. CAROLVS IX. DG. FRANCORVM REX. INVIC.; i. e., *Charles IX., by the grace of God, King of the French, unconquered.* 1572. Reverse, the King on his throne, under a canopy; VIRTVS IN REBELLES.† *Courage against Rebels.*

* The writer received them, in 1847 and after, from a valued correspondent then living in London, since deceased—Chas. Stokes, Esq., F. R. S. and F. S. A., eminent as an antiquary and numismatist. They are in perfect condition.

† *Virtus* is the word. Many a general who has shown desperate bravery would not have had the *courage* to butcher helpless women and children and unarmed men, even with Holiness behind, urging him on. The slaughter is variously estimated; probably about fifty thousand.

HUGUENOT MEDALS. REVERSE SIDE.

[illegible] Louis XIV [illegible]

[illegible] 1685 [illegible]

[illegible] alive [illegible] and it is not [illegible] to give a stri[illegible] ing from a [illegible] is also [illegible] a few months since the [illegible] Protestantism [illegible] the newspapers [illegible] it is not [illegible]

The [illegible] accustomed [illegible] with [illegible] cluded [illegible] no tolerance [illegible] exceptions [illegible] their [illegible] curses, terrify [illegible] dearer to them [illegible]

With these [illegible] Louis XIV [illegible]

[illegible] It is our pleasure [illegible] to meet [illegible]

It is plain that [illegible] or New Paltz [illegible] place of refuge.

[illegible] Louis [illegible] was a great [illegible]

[illegible] Medals. Reverse Side.

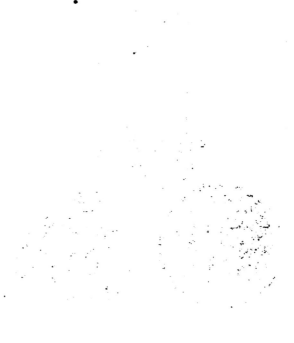

No. 3. Head of Louis XIV. LUDOVICUS MAGNUS* REX CHRISTIANISSIMUS. *Louis the Great, Most Christian King.* Reverse, RELIGIO VICTRIX. TEMPLIS CALVINIANORUM EVERSIS. MDCLXXXV. *Religion the Conqueress. Calvinist Temples Overturned.* 1685.

No. 4. Same head as No. 3. Reverse, OB VICIES CENT M. CALV. AD ECCL. REVOC. *On account of two million Calvinists recalled to the Church.* 1685.

Let it be said, once for all, that it is not well to keep resentments alive (as it is written, "Let all bitterness be put away"), and it is not for this purpose that these medals are inserted. It is to give a striking proof of the wisdom of our fathers in escaping from a dominion where such barbarities were enacted. It is also to give warning that the same spirit is alive. It is only a few months since the Papal See sent a demand to the Spanish King to suppress Protestantism. "This audacious demand," as the newspapers called it, is not likely to be complied with.

The laity, accustomed to mix with people of other persuasions, give and receive many tokens of human kindness. But the secluded priesthood, unknowing and unknown, held by no ties and no allegiance but the sacerdotal, are (with rare exceptions) like their Head at Rome; and, with their excommunications and curses, terrify the superstitious, and keep the mastery which is dearer to them than life.

With these Medals, we give the Edict of Louis XIV.

"It is our pleasure, that all the churches of the said pretended Reformed Religion, situate within our kingdom, shall be immediately abolished. We forbid our subjects of said religion any more to meet together in any place, or private house, for performing any part of their religion. And we renew our prohibition, that neither they nor their wives nor children do depart our dominions, nor transport their goods and effects, on pain of being sent to the galleys, for the men, and confiscation of bodies and goods, for the women."

IV.—THE PALATINATE OF THE RHINE—OLD PALTZ.

It is plain that Louis DuBois had much to do with the naming of New Paltz—"*le nouveau palatinat.*" It was in honor of his place of refuge.

* This Louis affected the distinction of *Le Grand Monarque*. One of his biographers, with a keen wit, remarks: "That he was a *great king*, all will agree. That he was a *great man*, is very doubtful."

The Count Palatine was, in theory, an officer of the Imperial Palace (*palatium*), whence came his title. He had also dominion over a considerable territory in Germany, which, however, was greatly reduced, as the result of wars, until, at the time when Louis went there, it was hardly as large as Ulster and Dutchess counties together, though much more populous. The sovereign was Charles Louis, grandson of James I. of England.

Those who visit the Mint, at Philadelphia, may see in its cabinet a large silver coin of this prince. The writer (not knowing now where he got it) placed it there many years ago. It is dated the very year when Louis left Europe (1660), and as the piece is extremely rare and in perfect condition, we may wonder whether he did not bring it with him as a pocket-piece, fresh from the Mint of Mannheim. It has on one side the head of the prince, with CAR. LVD. D. G. C. P. RH. S. R. I. ARCHITH. ET. EL. BA. DV. "Charles Louis, by the Grace of God, Count Palatine of the Rhine, Arch-Treasurer of the Holy Roman Empire, and Elector; Duke of Bavaria." On the reverse, three coats of arms, with the legend, DOMINUS PROVIDEBIT—"The Lord will provide."

This Holy Roman Empire, established by Charlemagne, who was crowned by the Pope A. D. 800, was by pretence a continuation of the ancient empire. It lasted until the great man died, and then the small men divided it. The imposing title was, however, kept up almost to our day.

V.—A FORTUNE MISSED.

For all whom it may concern, we insert the following remarkable narrative, which was sent to W. E. D. in 1854, by an unknown cousin in New York city. It is a translation of a letter which appeared in the *German Police Gazette* of that city:—

"*Amsterdam*, *Sept.* 4, 1854.—The attention of the happy Netherlands is drawn at present to a very interesting case of heritage. In the year 1704, died at Batavia, in Java, Jacques Du Bois, who was born at Vedrin, in the neighborhood of the Belgian city Namur, and left a fortune of twenty million florins.* He had no children, and willed in his legacy that the interest of his property

* About nine million dollars, present currency.

should be applied to the benefit of the Orphan Asylum of the city of Amsterdam for a term of fifty years.

"After the expiration of that time the capital was to be handed over to the legal heirs.

"In the year 1754 the moment had arrived when the hearts of the heirs, which had until then suffered 'Tantalus plagues,' should be gladdened. You may imagine that a handsome number of cousins came to light. Oh, cruel fate! The original document had been lost, and in the absence of an authentic copy the will could not be put in operation.

"So the matter rested a whole century. The cousins hoped in vain; and in place of gold, they could leave hope only to their heirs. But *tandem bona causa triumphat!* A happy accident has brought the will to light. Thirty-eight persons, mostly from Holland and Belgium, have been already acknowledged as legitimate heirs, and daily more announce themselves."

At the time when this article came to hand none of us knew that our ancestors sprang from a place only a few hours' ride from Namur, and that therefore it was probable this Jacques was of some kin to our Jacques and Louis, especially as it is evident that he was a Protestant, and had made his money under Dutch auspices.

So then, if any one of the tribe is disposed, at this late day, to spend some thousands of dollars in hope of getting part of it back, he has as good a start as we are able to give him, with our best wishes.

VI.—The Last Dwelling-place of Louis.

[From the Du Bois Record.]

In 1686, Louis left New Paltz, to finish his days at Kingston. He bought a house there from Derrick Schoepmes. This was undoubtedly the last house he lived in, and it was his residence for just ten years.

Some of his descendants will be pleased to have this spot identified. It stands at the corner of two streets where, in 1846, there was a store kept by Elijah Du Bois, overlooking the great meadow which was a pasturage in common for Kingston. It was left by will to Matthew, son of Louis, and by him conveyed, in 1731, to Matthew E. Thompson, who lived there to an extreme old age. In 1777, all the houses in Kingston were burned in one-half day by the British soldiery. Another house was erected on this lot, and the son of Mr. Thompson sold it, in 1787, to a Mr. Van Gansbeeck, from whom it passed to Elijah Du Bois. About 1816 the house gave place to a store.

The property continues to be owned by this esteemed cousin, who is a descendant of Matthew, above named, and was an active coadjutor in our reunion. He is the President of the National Bank of the State of New York, located at Kingston.

VII.—The Paltz Rock and Lake Mohonk.

No resident of the Paltz valley, nor any one named Du Bois, will think it out of place to insert in our book a picture of this commanding object. It was a corner-stone of the original purchase of the Paltz patentees.

Twenty-seven years ago, three of us, of whom Gilbert Du Bois was leader, accomplished what was then almost an exploit, though now it is an easy carriage-ride. We had to leave our horse and vehicle at a farm-house, half way up the mountain, and proceed on foot. We toiled upward through woods and rocks and occasional marshes, and without a path, knowing only that we must aim for the margin of a lake strangely situated almost at the top of the mountain. If the French settlers were ever there, they had an immense view of mountain ranges, but otherwise of monotonous forests, a little broken by meadows and Indian patches of cultivation. For us there was the lively addition of villages and chequered fields and farm tenements lying all around—a grand and beautiful panorama, to which no picture could do justice.

Little did we imagine that the day would come when this place, where huge rocks are wildly tossed about, would be converted into an elegant and favorite summer resort, and that two of us would sit in a bower looking down upon our daughters rowing a skiff upon the lake. Such a transformation has resulted from the enterprise and management of the Messrs. Smiley. And as if we had a special right there, our family name is often on their register of visitors.

VIII.—Rev. Benjamin Du Bois.*

[*From the Du Bois Record.*]

He was a son of the third Louis, and grandson of Jacob, and was born in Pittsgrove, N. J., March 30th, 1739. When a youth he inclined to the ministry, and received his education at Poughkeepsie, N. Y. He became pastor of the Reformed Dutch churches of Freehold and Middletown, Monmouth county, N. J., about the year 1764. He had his full share of ministerial difficulties. One arose from his desire to lay aside the Dutch language in preaching, which was resisted; another from the Tory influence during the revolutionary war; another from the opposition of his predecessor, who had been ousted for intemperance, but who had still his influential friends; and yet another from the raging of an excited controversy in his denomination for nineteen years, which produced its bitter fruits in his congregations. Yet such were the meekness and prudence of the good dominie that he rose above all these, retained the warm affection of his people to the last, and closed amongst them his useful life, in 1827, at eighty-eight years of age, and after a pastorate of sixty-three years, relieved during the last ten of these by the appointment of a co-pastor, and a competent support granted to him and his widow during life.

His ministry was faithful and successful; his sermons sound, evangelical and practical, and his zeal for the work so ardent that he kept on in very advanced life, although he sometimes would faint away in the pulpit, and his people often feared that he would die in the effort of preaching.

In the war of the revolution he sided actively with the patriots, commended the cause in his sermons and his prayers, and sometimes shouldered his musket and knapsack, and took his

* Always spoken of as "the Dominie," agreeably to Dutch usage. This title, from *dominus*, was applied to ministers in Holland, and to teachers in Scotland. They give the long sound to the *o*.

place in the ranks, to the great disgust of some of his Tory people and indignation of the British soldiery.

His wife was Phemertje (Phebe) Denise, a woman of intelligence and activity, sprightly, prudent and pious. She remained behind in this world until 1839, when she was almost ninety-six years old. They were very careful in the moral and religious instruction of their children, and had the happiness to see them all following their good example in the service of their Saviour, and transmitting even to the next generation the wholesome lessons of virtue, morality and religion which they themselves had received.

The dominie left ten children, five of whom emigrated to Franklin, Ohio, then a wilderness, whither quite a colony accompanied them, so that it received the name of the Jersey settlement; and a Presbyterian church which they soon established there (in the absence of a Reformed Dutch Classis) was called the Jersey church. Under the fostering care of these early settlers and of this church, this colony has grown up numerous, thriving, intelligent and religious.

IX.—Rev. Jonathan Du Bois.

BY R. P. D.

He was the son of Barent, and grandson of Jacob, and was born in Pittsgrove, N. J., December 3d, 1727. In his eighteenth year his attention was turned to the ministry, and he commenced his studies under the Rev. David Evans, pastor of the Pittsgrove Presbyterian church. Soon afterwards he was sent to the Classical Academy of the Synod of Philadelphia, at New London, Pa., under the care of Rev. Francis Alison. To enable him to pursue his studies, he was sent to his relatives at Esopus with a letter from his pastor, which throws much light upon the history and circumstances of the family and of the relation between the different branches in New Jersey and New York. It is endorsed, "A Petition on the behalf of Jonathan Du Bois, a hopeful beginner in learning," and is addressed "To all our Christian friends at Sopus, or anywhere else." He then recites that the bearer, along with his cousin John, the son of Louis Du Bois, his school-fellow, was pursuing hopefully his studies, but that his parents were not well able to bear the charges of his learning without assistance. He then earnestly begs that his near relations, and any others who were able, would open their hearts and hands and contribute to so good a work. He closes with several appropriate texts of Scripture, and by way of postscript adds: "Be it known to all whom it concerns, that the money which Barent Du Bois formerly collected at Sopus and elsewhere for our public religious affairs was honestly laid out according to the true tenor of the petition."

In a letter to his brother Jacob, from New London, November 24th, 1745, he says that in spite of the strangeness of the people, the place, the school and the master, and his rigid laws, he was getting on finely with his studies. Another letter to the same, dated Northampton, Bucks county, November 22d, 1750, which breathes throughout a very humble and pious spirit, speaks of having received a license to preach, and of entering upon his work. This was in the Dutch Reformed church of that place, in a settlement that was often called Holland, where as their pastor he spent the rest of his days. He was one of the first trustees of Queen's (now Rutgers) College in East Jersey. He was married to Eleanor, daughter of Nicholas Wynkoop, of Bucks county. He died December 15th, 1772, leaving four sons and four daughters. The eldest, Abraham, was a captain of cavalry during the revolutionary war. The youngest, Nicholas, became the teacher of the Young Ladies' Academy in Trenton, N. J., as well as ruling elder and chorister in the church of that place. These children of Jonathan intermarried with the Lefferts, the Wynkoops, and others of that region, and some of his posterity continue to reside in the southern parts of Bucks, or over the line in Montgomery.

X.—Benjamin Du Bois and Family, of Catskill, N. Y.

BY ANSON DU BOIS.

Benjamin Du Bois, second son and third child of Solomon, son of Louis, the Walloon, was "born at Pals" (New Paltz), and baptized at Kingston, May 16th, 1697. He married Catharine

Suylant, of Hurley, March 30th, 1721. A stone house built by the father-in-law, and replacing an older one, is still standing in good condition in Hurley street. Benjamin settled at Catskill, N. Y., about 1730, upon lot No. 1 of the Loveridge patent, which his father had purchased, in 1720, of Alexander McDowall, of Perth Amboy, N. J. In 1729 Benjamin bought lot No. 2 of the same pattern, except certain parcels previously conveyed, of Gysbert Lane. These lands had a water front on the Hudson river and on the Catskill and Katerskill creeks of some five miles, and a land line of three to four miles. It was a princely domain, and now comprises two villages, besides farms, water privileges and private residences of great value.

Our tradition places Benjamin's residence at Katerskill, two miles west of Catskill village, in the house given in our illustration. It was located, with an eye to trade, upon the great Indian trail between Catskill and the Schoharie. The house seems to have received two additions. The oldest part at the right was, no doubt, found standing, and first used by Benjamin, 1730, who probably added the middle section, and afterwards the left-hand section was built to afford needed room, and the middle doorway walled up. In a large stone at the top of this old doorway may be seen the date 1751, May 3, and the initials of Solomon, Cornelius and Benjamin in monograms.

Our Catskill settler, true to the great principles which had brought the family to America, was a religious man. He was an original member and officer of the old Catskill Dutch church formed in 1732, and signed the first call ever made by that church, February 8th, 1732, as a deacon, on Rev. George M. Weiss. Five years later he appears on the record as an elder. It is interesting also to know that he was ready to assist his neighbors. The old Reformed Dutch church of Caatsban, nine or ten miles south of Catskill, was built in 1732; and over the main door, which was then on the east side, were cut the initials of Benjamin Du Bois and his sons Solomon and Huybartus.

In old age Benjamin seems to have lived with his youngest son, Isaac, in West Catskill. His will was proved June 19th, 1767. He divides his lands between his sons Huybartus, Cornelius and Isaac, and his grandson Benjamin, son of Solomon, deceased. The daughters received portions in money, and to the widow was reserved ample support.

Our older people always spoke of the burial of Benjamin as a notable event. Great state was observed, and an entertainment unusually sumptuous closed the day. The phrase was always used, in describing the occasion, that "Benjamin was buried like a gentleman." He was interred at the top of the hill, a part of which appears at the right of the picture.

Benjamin Du Bois had four sons and two daughters who grew up—1. SARA, who married Christian Overbaugh. 2. SOLOMON, born 1724, married Margaret Sammons, of Brabant, September 27th, 1749, and died in middle life. He left three daughters and one son, Benjamin, who left issue; but his sons never marrying, the line is extinct except in the descendants of William E. Witteker and P. M. Eckler, who married daughters. 3. HUYBARTUS, born October 10th, 1725, survived the whole family. Married Cornelia Hallenbeck. He left four children—John, Lena, Rachel, Lydia and Treintje. 4. CORNELIUS, born November 12th, 1727; died June 5th, 1803; married Catharine Vanderpoel, of Kinderhook, September 21st, 1851. He was the most prominent of Benjamin's sons; a man of great activity and worth. He was an ardent Whig and a colonel of State troops in the revolution, and frequently in active service.

We are fortunate in having several honorable notices of our ancestor in "Simms' History of Schoharie County." Among the most important of these is one in regard to the part borne in opposing the raid of Sir John Johnson along the Mohawk valley, in October, 1780. General Van Rensselaer was in command of the Americans, but his dilatory measures annoyed his officers and men. At length, however, the British were overtaken a little above St. Johnsville by the advance under Colonel Du Bois, who immediately attacked, and a sharp engagement followed. Johnson was driven to a peninsula of the river, and in order to hold him there until Van Rensselaer came up, Du Bois took position on the north shore, next the British, while the gallant Colonel Harper closed in upon him with his Oneida Indians on the south. Van Rensselaer had given strict orders not to attack until he came up at the rising of the moon. But he did not come, and these advanced regiments had the mortification of seeing Johnson ford the river and escape. After the war it was reported that Johnson had determined to surrender, but that "Van Rensselaer did not give him a chance." The disappointed Americans denounced Van Rensselaer as a coward and traitor, and so deeply did this feeling take hold of them, that when once, in boyhood, I casually referred respectfully to the Van Rensselaers, my grandfather, who had probably been in his uncle's regiment at the time, became so exceedingly excited as to cause me the greatest surprise.

The house of Cornelius Du Bois was an asylum for those driven in from the back country during the war. The late Hon. John T. More, of Moresville, N. Y., enjoyed, with his father's family, this shelter. The Indians one night were preparing to capture Du Bois at his house, but were dissuaded by a neighbor. They took instead David and Anthony Abeel, from nearer the mountains. When the neighbor told Du Bois of this, after the war, the old hatred was too strong for concealment. "You saved my life," said Du Bois, "but you were a *Tory*, and *I could bear to kill you now.*"

At the surrender of Cornwallis, the patriots about Catskill assembled at the house of Col. Du Bois to celebrate the auspicious event. There was a great crowd, and long after midnight the frolic was maintained by the hilarious people. The house where this occurred was built by Cornelius in 1762, and is still standing.

Among Cornelius' sons, the oldest, Benjamin, was a student of Latin and Greek, his books still remaining, and well worn by use. There is a bit of romance connected with another son, Abraham. When a boy, a Scotchman named Peter Grant found Christian hospitality with his father. Grant's little girl Jennie impressed the susceptible heart of the lad, and when he grew up and wanted a wife he followed the emigrants to Delaware county, and married her.

One of their children, Grant Du Bois, is worthy of a more extended notice than can be here given. For seventeen years, from 1836 until his death in 1853, he served the American Tract Society, New York, and nearly all that time as missionary in charge of the Eleventh and Seventeenth Wards. He was a man of tact and efficiency. I will quote brifly from an extended notice of him by the late Rev. Dr. Murdock, of Elmira, N. Y.: "He was an earnest, original man, under the higher quality of genius. His thought and his power of description were of an order far above commonplace. His oral tales were equal to Dickens or Mayhew. Some who smile at this comparison have never heard him, in his retired moments, tell the adventures of a day, else the pathos, the piety and the genuine wit which excited tears and smiles and prayers would still be remembered, bearing out the allusion here made to the great masters of story-telling. His duty led him to traverse the worst districts of vice and misery, but he was equally welcome among the wealthy and refined. Perhaps to his parentage would some look for the key of his character,—pure Scotch, and genuine Huguenot. Both had suffered persecution from Rome, and here in the wilderness from them sprung a race with features of both, along with a dash of spirit peculiar to the land of their birth. Blessed is thy memory, Grant Du Bois. Blessed is many a garret and cellar of that great Babylon where tears are trickling down many an orphan's cheek for thee—many a widow weeps thy death." "We have this week," said a prominent elder of a New York church to the writer, "lost the two best men in New York, and one of them is Grant Du Bois."

Cornelius' third son, Barent, was a scout and ranger during the revolution, an intimate associate of Timothy Murphy, the famous Indian killer of that turbulent period. It was Murphy's unerring rifle that brought down the gallant General Fraser in the Burgoyne campaign, and Du Bois may have been with him at the time. In his later years he had many tales to tell of "Old Murphy," but was reticent of his exploits. Simms (Hist. Schoharie) says: "A black house was erected near Jacob Shafer's, in the spring of 1781, by Captain Du Bois of Catskill. This fort, with a small garrison, was for some time under the command of Captain Du Bois. I suppose this was Barent, who certainly operated in that region and received a pension from the government till his death, March 1st, 1837. Barent's son, Samuel, was well known in Greene county. He was for some time deputy, and finally high sheriff of the county. His son, Samuel Barent, is in our picture, sitting at ease at the left of his cousin William L., son of Grant. Through them we have rescued this relic of old times from oblivion. Another of Barent's sons named Barent settled in Alabama, and bought extensively in landed property at Montgomery, owning at one time a large part of the town. He bought also, largely, Indian lands. He accompanied General Jackson in several Indian campaigns, and was a government agent in removing the Indians of the south to the west of the Mississippi. He acquired great influence with the Indians, was made a chief by formal induction into office, and received an Indian name, *Posie Tchutco*, signifying *The Long Cat*—being unusually tall, well-made and agile. He married the daughter of a Creek chief.

5. ISAAC, born at Catskill, June 1st, 1831; married Lana Sammons, a sister of his brother Solomon's wife and of the Sammons brothers who were captured by the Indians. (See Stone's Life of Brant.) Isaac had two daughters, Eghje (Agnes) and Lana, and two sons, John and Joel. John's oldest son, Isaac, was a prominent citizen of Catskill. In 1812, with others, he built the first court house which was accepted by special Act of Legislature. The descendants of his second son, John D. or "Little John," are numerous and respectable. Ira, the fourth son, founded, in 1830, "*The Catskill Messenger*" newspaper, now the "*Catskill Examiner.*" He subsequently became clerk of the Board of Police, New York, and after long service retired, in age, on an annuity from that body.

Joel, born May 25th, 1762; died April, 29th, 1844. He participated actively in the revolution. He was a man of fine physique and enormous strength. Finding a cow one day sunk in a marsh, he seized her by the horns, and by sheer strength of arm dragged her forth to hard ground. Though decided and firm, he was a man of peaceful habits, an active member and officer of the Dutch church, and died a triumphant Christian death. He had three daughters. His only son, Isaac J. Du Bois, was born at Catskill, January 19th, 1789, but brought up in Orange county, where he married Catharine Hunter, and returned to Kiskatom, in his native township. In his youth he was fond of harmless fun, and many good stories are told of his early pranks. He passed clear through three drafts in the war of 1812. On one of these occasions he overheard the fatal numbers as they were clandestinely given the soldier next him, and might have thus been sure to draw clear himself. But this was not his way of doing business. He informed his father, then in command, who, with a stinging rebuke, ordered the offender under guard, and proceeded to make a new list of numbers. Early in his married life, Isaac J. was made permanently lame by a malignant disease in the right ankle. He was early elected Justice of the Peace, and held the office twenty-seven years. He was an ardent politician—a Federalist and Old Line Whig—and was solicited to become a candidate for the Assembly and other positions, but he refused to be anything other than "Squire Du Bois." He was a leading man in the Reformed Dutch church, a first elder in forming the church of Kiskatom from Leeds. He was modest, but of sound judgment, a great reader, of excellent memory, and possessed a reserve power of action and argument which few suspected until it was necessary to put it to use. He was always a farmer, and his portrait gives the right impression of him as a plain, but solid man. He died at Kingston, N. Y., October 3d, 1858, and was buried there beside his wife, who entered the better world only six months before him.

6. Treintje. This daughter of Benjamin Du Bois married John Van Orden; and, beside many worthy descendants by the name of Van Orden, she was grandmother of the late Rev. Dr. Jacob Van Techten, and of Rev. Samuel Van Techten, D. D., of Poughkeepsie, and of John Van Techten, Esq., now living at Leeds, N. Y., with unimpaired mind, at the venerable age of ninety years.

The descendants of Benjamin Du Bois, of Catskill, are to-day scattered over the whole country in honorable and useful positions. May they maintain the principles which make fragrant the memory of their ancestors!

XI.—Peter Du Bois and Some of his Descendants.

BY DR. JOHN COERT DU BOIS.

This ancestor of the Dutchess county branch of the family was born in Leyden, Holland, March 17th, 1674. He was the seventh child of Jacques Du Bois (brother of Louis, "the Walloon," of Ulster county, one of "the Twelve Patentees of the Paltz"), and Pierronne Bentÿn. According to the register of the Walloon church at Leyden, he was baptized on Sunday, March 18th, 1674. He was the last of the children of Jacques born in Holland, his younger brother, Christian, being born at Kingston, N. Y. He was only thirteen months old when his father emigrated with his family to America, and found a refuge in the rude settlement then called Wiltwyck, now the city of Kingston, N. Y., where his brother Louis had arrived fifteen years before. Jacques Du Bois died at Kingston about the year 1676.

Peter was married October 12th, 1697, to Jannetje Burhans. In the marriage record, in the Dutch language, still preserved at Kingston, he is described as a young man of Leyden, and his bride as a maiden of Brabant. Eleven children—seven boys and four girls—were born to them, six of whom married and had issue.

About the year 1707 he crossed the Hudson river to Dutchess county, and bought of Henry Beekman, the original patentee, a tract of land in what is now the town of Fishkill. This part of the country was then a wilderness; for we find that, in 1714, when his name is registered on the list of inhabitants of Dutchess county (then including Putnam county), the total population was only 445. But though this brave and hardy pioneer had to clear with his axe a spot in the dense forest for a home, yet our ancestors did not seem to think that a durable house could be built entirely of wood, for he made the walls of stone. Like most of the ancient Dutch houses, it had one story, low walls and a very steep roof. This old stone house still stands;—the superstructure is modern, but the same windows, set in deep embrasures, are seen—the same massive walls remain. It is situated about three-and-a-half miles east from Fishkill village, near a hamlet now called Swartwoutville, on the west side of Sprout creek, which stream ran through the centre of Peter's land.

The main part of the house consisted of a wide hall, sitting-room, parlor and bedrooms. The same hall stairs, leading to the upper floor, remained until quite recently, the wooden hand-rail supported by iron balusters. From the sitting-room three steps descended to a wing containing the kitchen and rooms for the negroes, and above a garret used for the storage of corn. The timbers in the wing supporting the upper floor were of cypress or white wood, of enormous size. A large stone fireplace, on one side of which was an oven, originally occupied the north side of the kitchen. This fireplace was of sufficient capacity to take in wood of the ordinary cord length, and high enough for a tall man to stand erect in it. During the long, cold winter evenings, Peter's negroes would sit on the ends of the back logs until the blazing fire would force them to retreat. This house remained unchanged for more than a century.

By his will, dated March 6th, 1735, Peter gave to his son Jonathan a farm on the east side of Sprout creek; and to Abraham and John lands on the west side, including the "Old Homestead." His other sons were provided with farms during his lifetime. In 1739 the old homestead, with the adjacent farm of 272 acres, was purchased from the other heirs for £330 by his son Christian. The deed is now in the possession of Henry Du Bois Baily, from whom most of the above facts have been derived. In this deed Christian is described as a "yeoman." He married Neeltje Van Vliet, and left two daughters and one son. He died about 1786, and his place of burial is unknown. His only son, Christian, Jr., born June 13th, 1746, inherited the homestead. In 1768 he married Helena Van Voorhees, and had eight children, seven of whom survived to mature age. He was a leading man in the community, and one of the prominent members of the building committee in the erection of the Reformed Dutch church at Fishkill village, in 1792. This edifice still remains, with its exterior unaltered, an ornament to the village. He died in 1807.

The "Old Homestead" then fell to his son Abraham, who, in 1812, made extensive repairs and alterations, adding another story of wood to the main building, and materially changing the interior, but leaving the old hall stairs with its peculiar rail. Abraham died, unmarried, May 12th, 1835. His elder brother, Coert, then purchased the old place. He had been born in it, but while yet a boy, after scanty educational advantages, had gone to New York city to enter upon a mercantile life. He was a clerk in that city during the great French revolution, and in after life often spoke of seeing the emigrant nobles landing in poverty on our shores, escaping only with their lives from the "Reign of Terror." He afterwards was a merchant in Fishkill and Rhinebeck, and by persevering industry, business skill, and, above all, scrupulous, honesty, gained a handsome competency. In 1801 he married Mary Thorn, of English ancestry, who bore him eight children, six of whom, five sons and a daughter, survived him. He was always an active and earnest member of the old whig party, and an ardent admirer of Henry Clay, and was noted through Dutchess and Columbia counties as an able advocate of the "American System of a Tariff for Protection." He was never an aspirant for political honors, but was repeatedly chosen supervisor of his town, and served in 1820–'21 as a member of the lower house of the State legislature. In 1836 his wife was stricken down with apoplexy, and remained until her death, ten years after, impaired in mind, and totally paralyzed in one-half of her body. In consequence of this affliction his home was broken up, and in the following year the "Old Homestead," after remaining in possession of Peter Du Bois and his direct descendants for 130 years, finally passed into the hands of strangers. Coert Du Bois died at the residence of his eldest son, Henry, in the village of Johnstown, Columbia county, N. Y., May 16th, 1854, at the ripe age of eighty years.

Peter Du Bois was a devoted Christian, and always a leader in that church with which, in early life, he became connected. In the church records of Kingston, Fishkill and Poughkeepsie, his name is prominent both as deacon and elder. We first find him on record as admitted to church-membership on confession of faith December 13th, 1696, on attaining his majority, and before his marriage; and in 1699 a liberal contributor for church purposes. When the Reformed Dutch churches of Poughkeepsie and Fishkill, forming a collegiate, were organized, in 1716, Peter Du Bois was one of the two first elders. In the third volume of the *Documentary History of New York*, page 974, will be found a petition, signed by him alone, "in behalf of the elders and deacons and other members of the Dutch Reformed Protestant Church of Fish creek, in Dutchess county, in the province of New York, to his Excellency, John Montgomerie, for permission to solicit aid to erect a church," dated June 28th, 1731. In the words of Gilbert Du Bois, a lineal descendant of his uncle, Louis, of Ulster, "He was the father of two churches; one at Poughkeepsie, the other at Fishkill. His faithfulness is fully proven by the records. For

Cornelius Du Bois.

more than twenty years his name appears as a prominent ruler of the two churches."

Peter Du Bois died in 1737, aged sixty-three, and his place of burial was unknown until recently. A few years ago some old tomb-stones in the Reformed Dutch church-yard in Fishkill village were re-set and scraped so that they could be deciphered. One, near Main street, all covered with moss, was thus restored, which proved to be the memorial of the last resting-place of our ancestor. The inscription is in the Dutch language, of which the following is a translation:—

"Here lies the body of Peter Du Bois, who departed this life the 22d day of January, in the year 1737–8, aged 63 years."

The death bears date both of the civil and the Gregorian year; the first ended March 25th, the latter December 31st, until 1752, when all dates were from the Gregorian year.

The descendants of Peter Du Bois are scattered over this broad land, but many still remain in old Dutchess, the chosen home of their ancestors, and in the adjoining counties.

XII.—Cornelius Du Bois.

BY DR. HENRY A. DU BOIS.

Cornelius Du Bois, copies of whose bust and portrait are here given, was the *fifth* of the name in America, and fourth descendant from Jacques Du Bois, the French Huguenot refugee.

He was born at Fishkill, in Dutchess county, N. Y., on the 20th of May, 1771. He was the youngest son of Peter Du Bois and Mary Van Voorhees, and grandson of Coert Van Voorhees and Catharine Fitkin.

When he was but twenty-five months old, his father, at the age of thirty-nine years, was thrown from his horse and killed, leaving his mother a widow with five children.

When five-and-a-half years old, his mother was remarried to Dr. Theodorus Van Wyck, Commissioner of Sequestration in the revolutionary war, a man of high character, a stern patriot, and of distinguished and influential family connections.*

*His nephew, General Theodorus Baily, was U. S. Senator, and his niece, Elizabeth Baily, married Chancellor James Kent.

Dr. Van Wyck had several children by a former marriage with Mrs. Du Bois' cousin, a daughter of Colonel John Brinckerhof. Two of his sons were General John B. Van Wyck, of Poughkeepsie, and General Abram Van Wyck, of Fishkill. Both of these maintained through life a strong personal regard for their younger step-brother, Cornelius, who was also their second cousin, and the latter of whom was always united to him in the bonds of an intimate and affectionate relationship. He had also two children by Mrs. Du Bois—Zephaniah Platt Van Wyck, who died in infancy, and Mary Van Wyck, who married Peter A. Mesier, Esq., of New York, a lovely and accomplished woman, to whom her half-brother, Cornelius, was always devotedly attached.

General Abram Van Wyck was Mr. Du Bois' favorite step-brother, and from him the writer of this memorial learned many incidents of his father's boyhood. "Your father (said the General) was a lad of great spirit and intelligence."

"He was always the leader in our juvenile sports. He possessed uncommon strength and agility. Although I was much larger and heavier than he was, he could put me on my back in a trice. He used to place a pole horizontally on the shoulders of two of us boys, and then going back for a start, would, in a bound, clear the pole, though nearly as high as his head."

In so large and mixed a family it is easy to conceive that matters were not always perfectly harmonious. Cornelius was the youngest member except his infant half-sister, Mary. He early manifested a proud, independent and self-reliant spirit, which made him the darling of his mother, but unfitted him to brook the wise restraint of a step-father. At the age of fifteen he read with avidity a sketch of the life of Benjamin Franklin, which so fired his youthful imagination, that he resolved to imitate his example, become a printer, and seek his fortune in New York.

This resolution he communicated to his mother, who was at first much distressed by it, but knowing the firm character of her son, she wisely acquiesced in it. She furnished him with money, and with a letter to her brother-in-law, Dr. Van Beuren, of Flatbush, L. I., and then with great sorrow and tremblings of heart, and with a fervent prayer to her Heavenly Father to guide and direct this, her favorite son, she gave him her parting embrace, the last he was destined to receive from her till he was recalled to her death-bed, one year afterwards.

Full of courage and hope for the future, the spirited lad started upon his journey, but as he pursued his lonely way, more solemn thoughts arose in his mind. He felt oppressed with the weight of responsibility which he had incurred by the wilful and hazardous step that he had taken. On the afternoon of the day on which he reached the city, weary and troubled in mind, he seated himself under the shade of a bush and communicated deeply with his own spirit.

His mother's blessing was upon him; he felt again her yearning embrace, and heard again her earnest entreaties that he would keep himself from evil courses and from evil men. He looked the future resolutely in the face, and realized the responsibility which rested upon him, in thus rashly exchanging the safety of a pious country home for the ensnaring allurements of a licentious city. He wept; but then and there under the shade of that lonely bush, he entered into a solemn engagement with himself, that rigid principles of right should always govern his conduct; that integrity and truth should be his guides through life, and that he "never willingly would do wrong." Then kneeling down, he fervently implored Almighty God to direct him in all his ways and enable him to fulfil what it was his fixed determination to attempt.

This firm resolution and this fervent prayer moulded the whole of his future life. God heard and answered it, as after events clearly proved; and the lad of fifteen arose, comforted and strengthened, to continue his journey to that city which was to be his earthly dwelling-place for all his future life, and where he attained to wealth and honorable distinction.

He was directed to the printing office of Francis Child, editor of a city newspaper. This gentleman was so much pleased with the appearance and bearing of the lad that he immediately took him into his employ, and also into his family. He continued to reside with Mr. Child from April, 1786, to January, 1787, when he was summoned to Fishkill to attend the death-bed of his mother. This fond parent had watched over her absent boy with anxious solicitude, and she had ascertained that there were young men in Mr. Child's office of dissipated habits and of dissolute morals. She could not die peacefully, leaving her beloved son exposed to such pernicious influences, and therefore she begged him to resign his position.

Cornelius unhesitatingly gave her the desired promise, though it nipped in the bud his cherished hopes of success in that line which he had selected.

Receiving his mother's thanks and dying embrace, he returned, after her death, to New York, where he found Mr. Child sick in bed, and announced to him his determination to leave his employ.

Mr. Child burst into tears, and said: "Cornelius, you are the only one in my office whom I can implicitly trust. I am often confined to my room by my ailment (severe attacks of gout), and if you leave me I know I shall be robbed. You are now sixteen years old; if you will stay with me till you are twenty-one, I promise you that I will take you into partnership."

This generous offer showed the great confidence which Mr. Child reposed in the capacity and integrity of his young clerk, and it must have proved a great temptation to an ambitious youth. His reply, however, was as follows: "Mr. Child, I thank you gratefully for all your past kindness to me, and I should be delighted to accept your present generous offer, if I felt at liberty to do so; but I promised my mother, on her death-bed, that I would quit your office, and no earthly inducement can make me break that promise."

With these words and with a sad heart he took an affectionate leave of this kind and generous friend, and went to the house of his uncle, Dr. Van Beuren, at Flatbush. While there he was attacked with the small-pox, and on his recovery he entered as clerk in the commercial house of his step-brother, of the firm of Sebring & Van Wyck, who then ranked among the prominent and wealthy merchants of New York.

He remained with them six years and two months, and during that time his clerkship was so entirely satisfactory to them, that when he left them to commence business on his own account they proffered him a written testimonial of his high character, with an offer to assist him pecuniarily in his future career.

In August, 1793, at the age of twenty-two years, he entered

into a co-partnership for ten years with Mr. Isaac Kip, to carry on the wholesale grocery and commission business, under the firm-name of "Kip & Du Bois." They occupied the three-story brick store No. 36 Front street, which is still standing and in the possession of one of his daughters, to whom he bequeathed it by will.

This business, conducted under a written engagement of the partners with each other, to be "prudent, industrious and honorable in all our transactions," prospered beyond the most sanguine expectations of either of them.

In 1803, when the partnership expired, Mr. Kip retired with a competency, and Mr. Du Bois was able to purchase the store No. 36 Front street, with the lot running back to Water street. This store he continued to occupy till 1829, a period of thirty-six years, when he built a much larger store and warehouse on the rear lot, known as No. 37 Water street, which he occupied till he retired from business, February 15th, 1840. This building is also still standing, and in the possession of his other daughter, to whom he, in like manner, left it by will.

On the 11th of April, 1803 (just previous to his dissolution with Mr. Kip), Mr. Du Bois married Sarah Platt Ogden, a descendant, on the paternal side, from the old and distinguished Ogden family of New Jersey, and on the maternal side from the equally old and respectable family of the Platts.

The writer of these pages (which are designed solely to meet the eye of kindred) must be permitted to pause for a moment in the record of his father's life, in order to pay a passing tribute to the memory of his sainted mother.

Mrs. Du Bois was one of those rare persons to whom the words of Halleck might be literally addressed, and with the strictest truth—

"None knew thee but to love thee,
Nor named thee but to praise."

To great personal beauty, she united a very winning and affectionate manner and the disinterested loveliness of a pure Christian character. It was proverbial to say of her, that she was "the sunbeam" of every circle she entered.

Such was her nice, delicate tact, her sweet sympathetic nature and Christian *charity*, which knew no guile, that she seldom failed in her effort to improve or *gladden* every person who came in contact with her, even for an hour. She sedulously endeavored to impress on her children the duty of embracing every opportunity to do some good to all around them, rich or poor, friend or stranger, and to strive that each one might be better, or at least happier, from their intercourse, however short or casual.

Her private personal acts of benevolence were unceasing and very extensive. Many pensioners, unknown to her family during her life, mourned her death; and many who, through her patronage and timely aid, had attained to position and competency, came forward, after her decease, to acknowledge the fact, and declare that her name was a household word in their families.

After her death, Mr. Du Bois computed that her *private* charities, during their married life, amounted to $100,000. He stated, that though sometimes annoyed at not being always made cognizant of, and a participator in, these charities, "Yet," said he, "I firmly believe that every dollar thus spent by her has been blessed to me and my children." He would also add, "Her very faults (if she had any) always leaned to virtue's side." She died in the city of New York, on the 15th of March, A. D. 1836, in the fifty-fifth year of her age. Her memory is embalmed in the hearts of her children, and of many others still living, but her true "record is on high."

We now return to the subject of our Memoir. Mr. Du Bois, by his marriage with Sarah Platt Ogden, had five surviving children, viz:—

1st. Mary Elizabeth; married to Francis Potter, of New York, and after his death, to Edward S. Gould, son of Judge Gould, of Litchfield, Connecticut.

2d. Henry Augustus; married to Helen, daughter of Peter A Jay, Esq., and granddaughter of Chief Justice John Jay.

3d. Cornelius; married to Mary Ann, daughter of John Delafield, Esq., of New York.

4th. Sarah Platt; married to Dr. Alfred Wagstaff.

5th. George Washington; married to Maria, daughter of the Rt. Rev. Charles P. McIlvaine, Bishop of Ohio.

These children are all now alive, with numerous children and grandchildren.

Although somewhat out of order in this record, we cannot refrain from giving here an illustration of Mr. Du Bois' deep religious feeling, a trait which marked his whole life, though never ostentatiously displayed.

We find among the many loose memoranda which he was accustomed to make in regard to the incidents of his life, and from which this Memoir is principally compiled, the following statement, under date of March 17th, 1834, six years previous to his retirement from business: "I have brought up and expensively educated five children, three sons and two daughters [all grown up except the youngest, a lad eleven years old], from the fruits of an early and close application to business, carefully and prudently managed to the present period. I expect, if nothing unforseen happens, to leave them and their families in easy circumstances, provided they pursue the same course as regards their worldly concerns. As for the higher and more enduring treasures of another and better world, 'it is not mine to give,' nor is it *my* example that I wish them to follow. I leave them in the hands of that Heavenly Parent, who can do more and better for them than any earthly father. *His* choicest blessing is invoked in their behalf whose tender mercies and loving kindness have followed me and them all our days, and in whom let us put our trust and confidence for the life that is to come; not for any merits of our own, but resting our hope entirely on the merits of Redeeming Love; on Him who died for us, that we might hereafter live in glory: To whom be praise forever more."

CORNELIUS DU BOIS.

We again return to the order of our record. After Mr. Du Bois had dissolved partnership with Mr. Kip, he continued for twenty years, viz: to 1823, to do business alone, and with very successful results. During this period, he was solicited by Mr. John Enders, of Richmond, Va., one of the founders of the "manufactured tobacco" business in Virginia, to act as his agent for the sale in New York of the tobacco manufactured by him. This he consented to do, and, gradually dropping his wholesale grocery business, he applied all his resources to an extensive prosecution of this commission business on behalf of Mr. Enders, and most of the other large manufacturers in Virginia, who were solicitous that he should act as their agent also.

In this connection there is one fact which deserves notice, as showing their high appreciation of Mr. Du Bois' character.

When he had consented, at Mr. Ender's solicitation, to this change of business, he told him that he would take charge of and manage his property and that of his friends in Virginia just the same as if it were his own. He would sell on short credits and to the best of his judgment, but that he would not in any case *guarantee* a sale. If he made a bad debt he would remit his commission, but the eventual loss must fall on the owner. This point, which was conceded to him, and to which he adhered during the whole subsequent career of his commercial life, made him perhaps at that time the only exception among commission merchants in the city of New York, and certainly the only exception among the many tobacco commission merchants who afterwards sprang up in the city as his rivals and competitors in that branch of trade. Such was the implicit confidence reposed in the business capacity and perfect integrity of Mr. Du Bois, that almost every one of the original manufacturers adhered to him despite the offers of wealthy firms to guarantee their sales. Mr. Du Bois, unmoved, adhered to his principle, and his Virginia friends adhered to him; but when he retired his successors were obliged to conform to the universal custom of guaranteeing sales. He had, previous to his retirement from business, taken into his firm his son Cornelius Du Bois, who was educated for the bar, and was successfully prosecuting his profession in connection with Edgar S. Van Winkle, Esq., with whom he had been associated in practice for four years.

He relinquished his profession at the instance of his father, who was desirous that a son should succeed him having his own name, which, for nearly half a century, had been known and honored by business men. He succeeded to his father's firm and business, but he could not, however, adhere to the business policy which his father had maintained for forty-seven years, but was forced to accept the then universally recognized rule of commission merchants, and guarantee all sales.

In 1823, Mr. Du Bois contemplated retiring from business, having realized an ample fortune, but from a kind wish to benefit one of his clerks, whom he had brought up in his firm from boyhood and for whom he entertained the sincerest regard, he determined to continue, and to employ his capital in the business for their joint benefit.

In another memorandum, dated May 3d, 1827, giving some incidents of his life, he says: "I continued alone in business and on my own account from 1803, when I dissolved with Mr. Kip, to the spring of 1823, a period of twenty years, and thirty years from my commencement in 1793.

"I had thoughts of retiring altogether from mercantile business on the earnings of a life devoted so long to its pursuits, but as my commission business had proved profitable, safe and increasing, and being desirous of benefiting the interests of a young man whom I had brought up, and who had served me faithfully for a long time, I agreed to give Isaac A. Storm an interest, under the firm of 'Cornelius Du Bois & Co.,' for seven years from March, 1823, which firm now exists, and will expire by its limitation on the 15th of February, 1830, when I shall have been (if I survive) thirty-seven years in business."

Mr. Storm, after Mr. Du Bois' retirement, took his patron's son into partnership, and became the senior partner in the firm of "Storm, Du Bois & Co;" and when this firm was succeeded by that of "Du Bois & Vandervoort," he still evinced an interest in the junior firm, and retained a desk in their counting-room, being unwilling to sever entirely his connection with the old ship in which he had sailed from boyhood, and for whose owner and first master he always felt the greatest reverence.

Mr. Storm was a man of sterling integrity, of untiring industry and of great business capacity. By strict economy and by adhering to the maxims in which Mr. Du Bois had trained him from boyhood, he amassed a fortune of a half-million of dollars, the justly-earned reward of a life-long devotion to the business interests of his revered friend, and of many others, who, with implicit confidence, entrusted property to his care and disposal.

On the 15th of February, 1840, Mr. Du Bois closed his commercial career. For forty-seven years he had continuously carried on an extensive and prosperous business without failure. But few merchants in the city of New York can show such a record. No note of his had ever remained unpaid at maturity. His commercial paper was never, to his knowledge, but in one instance, submitted to a *shave* beyond the ordinary discount. In that instance, the writer of this Memoir was concerned, during the hard times of 1836–'37, and well does he remember the indignation of his father when apprised of the fact.

Active benevolence was a prominent trait of Mr. Du Bois' character. While burdened with the cares of an extensive business, he nevertheless gave a great deal of his time and money to various public institutions and charities. We find a memorandum in his hand-writing, dated January, 1824, giving a list of the societies with which he was then connected, requiring almost daily attention. The list is as follows:—

The Chamber of Commerce,	A Member.
Union Bank,	A Director.
Fulton Fire Insurance,	A Director.
Do. do. do.	Chairman of the Loaning Committee.
Savings Bank, Chambers street,	A Trustee.
Pauperism Society,	A Manager.
Mariners' Church Society,	A Manager and Vice President.
Humane Society,	A Manager and Treasurer.
House of Refuge,	A Manager, Treasurer and Vice President.
New York Hospital,	A Member—formerly a Governor.
Eye Infirmary,	A Member.
New York Public School,	A Trustee.
New York High School,	Treasurer and Trustee.
Emigration of Free Blacks to Hayti,	A Member.

He was largely instrumental in the success of the Humane Society, and in founding the House of Refuge for Juvenile Delinquents. The Humane Society was established in 1787, for the purpose of relieving poor debtors in the city prison. When the Act for the imprisonment of debtors was abolished, the Society was temporarily continued for the relief of urgent cases of distress in the city. Its organization comprised many of the most prominent citizens of New York.

Its officers were—John Adams, President; Benjamin Bailey, Vice President; Cornelius Du Bois, Treasurer; Anthony I. Bleecker, Secretary. And its managers were—James Bleecker, Lynde Catlin, George Griswold, John Haggerty, Joseph Kernochan, Stephen Whitney, James Boyd, I. W. Francis, M. D., James Lovett, Jacob Morton, John McComb, Peter I. Nevius, John Outhout, Benjamin L. Swann, H. F. Sewall, Nat. Weed, Thomas Suffern.

Mr. Du Bois acted as treasurer of this society for eighteen years, when it became defunct by the non-election of officers, leaving, with accumulated interest, the sum of $2000 in his hands.

After many efforts to get a legal meeting of its members to dispose of this money, Mr. Du Bois presented a petition to the legislature to authorize him to distribute this sum of $2000 among certain charitable and needy institutions. An Act was accordingly passed, May 11th, 1840, entitled "An Act for the Relief of Cornelius Du Bois, of New York," authorizing him to make this distribution. Few treasurers now-a-days would go to the same trouble and expense to rid themselves of unreclaimable funds left in their hands, but he was not one to rest satisfied with any trust-account unclosed.

The House of Refuge for Juvenile Delinquents was Mr. Du Bois' *pet* charity. He was one of the original founders of this noble institution. While in health, he visited it every week, minutely inspected every part of it, and generally took one or more of his children with him, in order to inspire them with charity for those poor young outcasts from society, who, being deprived of the family blessings which they enjoyed, had become transgressors of the law.

In this connection the following incident elucidates the character of the man:—

The institution at one time stood in great need of means. Mr. Du Bois undertook to go among his commercial friends and personally solicit aid. He called upon Mr. L., a wealthy and benevolent man, somewhat his senior in years, and who had always been a liberal contributor. To his utter amazement, Mr. L. refused to give a cent. Mr. Du Bois eyed him silently for a few moments, and then said: "Mr. L., if either you or I have anything to do for our Master, we have no time to lose. I wish you a very good morning." The rebuke was felt, and in the afternoon of the same day his conscience-stricken friend sent him a very generous donation.

On the occasion of his death, the Directors of this institution met, and passed resolutions deeply lamenting their loss. How keenly they recognized it, will appear from the letter of the Secretary, and the resolutions of the Board of Managers enclosed in said letter, a copy of which is appended to his Memoir.

Mr. Du Bois' character was of no ordinary type. His intelligence was extraordinary, and his judgment of men and things almost infallible. His integrity was inflexible, and his maintenance of what he thought right, fearless and immutable. Truth, duty and honor were to him sacred things, never to be trifled with. One of the earliest lessons impressed by him upon his sons, was "Speak the truth. Do your duty, and let your motto be, *Death before dishonor.*" It may perhaps be said that he had a somewhat proud, self-reliant spirit of independence; but this was tempered by great natural delicacy and refinement of sentiment, by courteous manners, and by a kind and generous heart. But the great underlying substratum of his character is to be found in his quiet, unostentatious, but deep religious sentiment and firm trust in God. "The fervent prayer under the bush," and the consequent firm resolve of the lad of fifteen, moulded the whole future life of the man, and made him what all acknowledged him to be, "*integer vital sceleris que purus.*"

We will close this imperfect Memoir with two incidents of which we have been reminded, and to the truth of which we can testify from other sources. My informant writes: "The following, which occurred at the commencement of his mercantile career, will serve to illustrate his Christian firmness and resolute character. After he had risen to a position of prominent responsibility in the counting-house of Sebring & Van Wyck, a position which insured him a good salary, he had to encounter a trial which put his moral firmness to a severe test.

"Several young men of his acquaintance, who occupied similar positions in other counting-houses, had formed a club, and were in the habit of spending their evenings at their club-rooms in card-playing and low-bred convivality. Their invitations to him to join them were persistent and importunate to such a degree, that he resolved at last to adopt a course which should put an end to these annoying solicitations. So, on one occasion, as they passed the store, just as he was about closing it, they renewed their pressing invitations as usual, with taunting remarks; whereupon he consented to meet them at their club-rooms at the appointed hour that same evening. He found them assembled and seated at their card-tables, while from a bar in the adjoining room waiters were bringing in glasses of liquor. Profane expressions were frequently used, amid ribald jests and witticisms and senseless merriment. At his entrance he was warmly welcomed, and when seated, a glass of liquor of some sort was placed before him, and he was informed that, in accordance with their established custom, he must, as an *initiate*, drink the health of the company, and offer a toast. 'But, gentlemen,' said Mr. Du Bois, 'I have made it a rule to abstain altogether from intoxicating drinks, and I beg you will excuse me, and let me be a looker-on.' 'This is out of the question,' the chairman replied, with an air designed to intimidate. 'No one can enter or leave these rooms without conforming to our inviolable custom. If you refuse, you will take the consequences.' 'Then,' said Mr. Du Bois, rising as he spoke, 'under protest against such an exaction, I offer you the following sentiment. I consider you very suitable companions for each other, but not fit associates for me, nor for any one who has a decent regard for morality and self-respect.' So saying, he placed the glass, untasted, on the table. Angry exclamations followed, with a sudden threatening movement towards him, but his powerful and commanding person, his perfect self-possession and his bright eye, kindling with indignation, conveyed to their minds a wholesome fear of the consequences, should they attempt by personal violence to resent his language. So wishing them a good evening, he withdrew unmolested."

The other instance is as follows: When Cornelius Du Bois commenced business on his own account, he applied to one of the city banks for the usual temporary accommodation.

The firm of Kip & Du Bois was, of course, unknown in business circles, and for this reason their paper was thrown out in the meeting of the board of directors.

Mr. Isaac Sebring, with whom Mr. Du Bois had been clerk for the six years just preceding this application, was at that time one of the bank directors, and taking up the rejected paper he placed his initials on the corner of it ("riding it," as it was technically called), thereby assuming some individual responsibility in regard to it, and the accommodation was then voted. The paper was promptly met at maturity, and from that time the firm of Kip & Du Bois encountered no difficulty in obtaining discounts at that bank for any required amount. Mr. Du Bois left that he owed a debt of gratitude to Mr. Sebring for his timely aid, and for the friendly confidence which it implied, and it was one of his prominent characteristics never to forget a kindness.

Some years after this, Mr. Sebring was drawn into speculations in large real estate operations by a plausible, crafty and adventurous speculator. They purchased together the lots immediately north of the city park, and erected thereon a large and expensive building, afterwards well known as Washington Hall. Mr. Sebring had such entire confidence in the perfect integrity of his partner in these speculations, that, confining his attention to his own legitimate business, he left everything, without suspicion, to the management and control of his associate. He endorsed notes to large amounts without sufficient caution, and as a consequence he became irretrievably embarrassed. In the hope, however, of struggling through if only he could get temporary relief, he presented his note to a city bank for discount. The note was unhesitatingly thrown aside, because of the well-known fact that he was involved beyond the possibility of recovery. The bank directors, while refusing his paper, expressed freely and sincerely their sympathy for him, for he was well-known and highly esteemed among business men for his industry, his enterprise and his scrupulous honesty. Mr. Du Bois had, meanwhile, risen to the highest mercantile position. His business had been wonderfully prosperous, and enlarged under his judicious and sagacious management. He was at this time *one of these bank directors*. Taking up Mr. Sebring's rejected paper, he, to the astonishment of his colleagues, *endorsed* it with his full name to give legal validity to its responsibility. Nor was he at all surprised when, at the maturity of the paper, he found himself obliged to take it up.

Mr. Sebring, for years after this occurrence, even to the end of his life, continued to receive from Mr. Du Bois constant substantial proofs of his firm friendship and lasting gratitude for this comparatively small but timely aid, and for his unvarying kindness to him during his clerkship, as well as for his generous offer to assist Mr. Du Bois when he left him to commence business on his own account.

Cornelius Du Bois died at Saratoga Springs (his usual summer resort), on the 8th day of September, A. D. 1846, in the seventy-sixth year of his age.

Although he had been suffering from a painful malady for several months, yet his death happened so unexpectedly that some of the members of his family, who were away from home, or who lived at a distance, were unable to reach him in time to close his eyes. His son Cornelius, and his youngest and favorite son, the Rev. George Washington Du Bois, and a faithful body servant, were the only ones present at his death.

He died as he had lived, with humble but firm trust in his God and Saviour. He had often remarked to his daughter Mary, that he did not fear being dead, but that he shrank from what he supposed might be the agony attending the parting of the soul from the body. His disease was a painful one, and at this time he was a great sufferer, but at the last he was vouchsafed an easy and peaceful death. On the afternoon preceding his death, he said: "If it is God's will, I am ready to go to-night;" and then speaking of the God who had protected his youth and guided him through life, he said: "He will not forsake me now that I am old and grey-headed."

His life was a perfectly well-proportioned and *well-rounded* one, fulfilling with strict rectitude every duty in that sphere in which God had placed him.

To such a life, though unmarked by any striking achievement or glaring worldly distinction, may be applied the words of the Master: "Well done, good and faithful servant; thou hast been faithful over a few things, I will make thee ruler over many things; enter thou into the joy of thy Lord."

The following is in the letter enclosing the resolution of the Board of Managers of the Society for the Reformation of Juvenile Delinquents:—

CORNELIUS DU BOIS, Esq.

Dear Sir:—I have been directed to convey to the family of your late father a copy of preamble and resolution adopted at a meeting of the Board of Managers of the Society for the Reformation of Juvenile Delinquents, held on the evening of the 7th instant. I therefore enclose them to you, with a request that you will present them to your family.

Participating with the board in their deep sense of the loss the institution has sustained, I beg leave to offer to you my sincere sympathy under this afflicting dispensation of Providence.

The long life of your venerated father having been faithfully and zealously devoted to the promotion of objects of public charity and benevolence, his loss will be deeply felt, and more particularly by his associates, the Managers of the House of Refuge, who were the witness of his benevolent exertions in the cause of suffering humanity.

Accept, dear sir, the assurances of the sincere regard of

Your very obedient servant,

NEW YORK, October 8, 1846. JOHN H. GOURLIE.

RESOLUTION.

At a meeting of the Board of Managers of the Society for the Reformation of Juvenile Delinquents, held October 7th, 1846, the following preamble and resolution were unanimously adopted:—

WHEREAS, Since the last meeting of the Board of Managers it has become their painful duty to record the decease of their respected associate, Cornelius Du Bois, Esq., one of the Vice Presidents of the Society, who died at Saratoga Springs, on Tuesday, the 8th of September last. Mr. Du Bois was one of the *original* projectors of this Society, and early took a lively and active interest in its formation.

In the collection of funds to assist in its organization, he was one of a number of very efficient and benevolent gentlemen who devoted much time to this object, and, by introducing economy in expenditure and order in its arrangements, were indefatigable in their efforts to place it on the high ground it has attained.

To the unwearied exertions of these gentlemen, many of whom have gone to their final reward, and but few are left to aid us by their counsels and advice, the great success and usefulness of the institution may be mainly attributed.

For eighteen years Mr. Du Bois held the office of Treasurer, and many of the present members of the board can bear testimony to the faithfulness and untiring industry which he devoted to its duties, permitting nothing to be neglected which fell to the province of that office to attend to. His interest in the welfare and success of the Society in no way diminished until declining health compelled him to retire from active duty, and then his interest continued unabated while he lived, and his good wishes for its continual success and usefulness were frequently and warmly expressed.

The Board of Managers, feeling sensibly the loss of so valued a member, and one who has contributed to much to advance the object for which it was established, have therefore—

Resolved, That the foregoing be entered on the minutes of the proceedings to the Society, and that an attested copy be transmitted to the family of the deceased, expressing their sympathy and condolence with them under the melancholy bereavement they have sustained by this dispensation of divine Providence.

COPY OF A CARD PUBLISHED IN NEW YORK IN JANUARY, 1831.

The Humane Society return their thanks to those charitable persons who have hitherto contributed towards the benevolent purposes of the institution, and beg leave to state to them that in the course of the last year, the Society has furnished food to the poor debtors confined in prison, by supplying them with good soup and a due proportion of meat and bread.

In addition to the soup issued to the prisoners, a considerable quantity has been given to such poor persons as have applied for it at the Soup House.

As their funds are now nearly exhausted, they are induced once more to appeal to the benevolence of their fellow-citizens; and they feel themselves justified in trusting that the same spirit of human kindness, in which the Society have hitherto found so ample and so liberal a supply, will be ever ready to meet the future demands; and though an opinion seems to prevail in the community that some charitable institutions give a direction to the feelings of humanity unfavorable to frugality and honest industry, yet to the efforts and objects of this Society no such consequences can ever attach. The humble meal dealt out to the lonely prisoner can be no inducement to him to remain within his prison walls; nor can the homely fare afforded by the Society to the calls of hunger, give indulgence to sloth, or weaken the motives to industrious exertion. Necessitous and humble must he indeed be who, in either case, solicits and receives that boon of charity.

It is for unfortunate beings, who, to the wretchedness of poverty, have added the misery of being immured in a prison, or being shut out from the comforts of social intercourse, and for whose support no provision is made by the laws of the land. It is to give sustenance to the poor, who are asking for food, that we now solicit your further aid.

Thus far, and for a period of more than forty years, has this institution been supported solely by the benevolence of a feeling community; nor is that fund exhausted. We feel and know, that to those amongst us to whom a kind Providence has given the ability, it has also given the heart to contribute to the relief of human wretchedness.

Donations in any article of food will be thankfully received at the Soup House, and in money by any of the members of the Society.

JOHN ADAMS, *President.*
BENJAMIN BAILEY, *Vice President.*
CORNELIUS DU BOIS, *Treasurer.*
ANTHONY BLEECKER, *Secretary.*

(Here follow the names of the managers as contained in the Memoir.)

XIII.—Peter K. Du Bois

Died at his residence in Pleasant Valley, Dutchess county, N. Y., on the 30th March, 1872, at the age of seventy-six years. He occupied a prominent place in the history of the State, and it is a matter of regret that we have not more details.

The sterling integrity and sound judgment which were marked traits of his character, early called the attention of his fellow-citizens to his fitness as the recipient of delegated trusts, and it may be safely said of him, that he never disappointed his constituents.

In the year 1842 he was called to represent his district in the Assembly of this State, where his ready comprehension of legislative duty, simplicity yet force of character, and earnestness of purpose in whatever he engaged, gave weight and influence to his position.

In 1846 he was, with great unanimity, elected to the Constitutional State Convention, and took a prominent part in the proceedings of that body for revising the organic law of the State. He possessed in an eminent degree the qualities of mind and character essential to the responsible services required. He was the type of a class of men who saw the wants of popular government, and exhibited single-minded devotion in purpose and action.

In later life Mr. Du Bois remained upon his farm, in the successful pursuit of that occupation, where those who had the pleasure of his conversation were impressed with his extensive and thorough knowledge of the past and present history of the country.

At home, and among his neighbors, his life was such as to win lasting love and respect, and we but record a general sentiment in adding, that citizenship, as illustrated by such men, meets and answers its noblest ends. To the last he retained his strength of intellect and kindly interest in the welfare of others. An organic disease of the heart, with which he had been for some time affected, at length closed his eyes in final rest.

XIV.—Capt. Theodore Bailey Du Bois, U. S. N.

BY EGBERT DU BOIS.

He was the son of Thomas K. Du Bois, and was born in New York city, in 1823.

His parents died while he was yet a boy; and after a few years spent on the farm with his uncle in Dutchess county, at the age of sixteen, he adopted the sea as his calling. He never left it permanently till incapacitated for duty, and within about a year from his death.

He rose rapidly in his profession; was an accomplished navigator, and a favorite with ship-owners; attained a command early in life, and was in some of the best employs of New York and Boston. He was never a day out of a command except at his own desire.

About the year 1855, while in command of the new clipper ship, *Shooting Star*, owned by Samuel G. Reed & Co., of Boston, he entered the port of Bangkok, Siam, his being the first ship of a civilized nation entering that country, after her ports had been opened by treaty to the commerce of the world. He was hospitably entertained by the king and government, receiving from them some rare and costly presents. He afterwards sold his vessel to them, and returned home a passenger.

Soon after the outbreak of the late war he was admitted as a commissioned officer of the navy, direct from the merchant service. Though this was an unusual course, he was held in great esteem by the navy officers who became acquainted with him. In 1862 he held the rank of Lieutenant-Commander, and was in command of the *Albatross* when lashed to the Hartford, the flagship of Admiral Farragut, when she passed through the storm of shot and shell from Port Hudson. For frequent acts of coolness, bravery, and for excellent seamanship, Captain Du Bois received the thanks and commendations of Admiral Farragut in an autograph letter, which is now carefully preserved by his family.

After the close of the war he was employed by the government to pilot to their destination the two iron-clads, monitors, which had been sold to the Peruvian government; and immediately after one to Japan, sold to that government. His letters to the New York *Herald*, during these eventful trips, were highly appreciated, and published regularly by that paper.

In 1872 he commanded the steamship *Bahia*, in the Brazilian Navigation Company, in employ of Garrison & Co., of New York, till the discontinuance of that line.

His last command was the steamship *Suffolk*, laying cable in the West Indies, in employ of the Western Union Telegraph Company.

In the fall of 1873, while his vessel was under repairs in Baltimore, slight aberrations of mind were observed by his friends, and soon his physicians discovered unmistakable signs of softening of the brain, suggesting, as its remote cause, injuries received on board the iron-clad *Osage*, in the employ of government, immediately after the war. The malady grew rapidly upon him, and terminated in death December 13th, 1874, aged fifty-two.

XV.—Koert Du Bois.

BY CORNELIUS DU BOIS, OF STATEN ISLAND.

Koert Du Bois, whose portrait is here inserted, was the eldest son of Peter Du Bois and Mary Van Voorhees. He was a brother of Cornelius Du Bois, of New York, and the grandfather of Captain Theodorus Bailey Du Bois, whose memoirs are herein recorded.

He was born January 25th, 1763, and lived and died on his patrimonial estate at Clinton, afterwards known as Pleasant Valley, in Dutchess county, N. Y.

He was married February 5th, 1786, to Elizabeth Burroughs, by whom he had eight children.

1st. Mary, born 28th February, 1787; married to James Odell.
2d. Elenor, born 7th November, 1789; married to Dr. Lewis Ring.
3d. Thomas, born 22d April, 1792; married to Sarah Corwin.
4th. Peter K., born 27th March, 1796; married to Sarah Lattin.
5th. Eliza, born — March, 1799; married to James Congdon.
6th. Cornelius, born 9th July, 1802; married to Julia Ann Moore.
7th. Robert K., born 4th May, 1805; married to Mary Conklyn.
8th. Jane Ann, born 15th December, 1807; died at eight years of age.

Koert Du Bois was tall of stature, and of commanding presence, quiet in manner, gentle in life, honorable, conscientious and upright in all his dealings. With his wife, who was his true yoke-fellow and loving helpmeet, he embraced the religious principles and doctrines of the Society of Friends. They both continued through life devoted and honored members of that denomination. The name of Quaker, like that of Huguenot, was at first given in derision, but like it also, it was made, by the heroism and noble lives of those who accepted it, a name of honor and renown.

But the Quaker differed from the Huguenot in this respect, that he denied a right to the followers of the meek and lowly Jesus to take up arms and shed the blood of his fellow-man in defence of their rights. His religion taught him to obey the divine injunction recorded in the Sermon on the Mount: "I say unto you, love your enemies, bless them that curse you, do good to them that hate you, and pray for them which despitefully use you and persecute you."

His only war-cry was as expressed in the lines of the poet Hosmer—

"Up! fearless battlers for the Right!
And flood old groaning earth with light;—
Bid nations ponder well, and pause
When blade corrupt Ambition draws!
O, teach the world that conquest wears
A darker brand than felon bears!
Prolific fount, from earliest time,
Of Murder, Orphanage and Crime."

In the character of Koert Du Bois, the inflexible traits of the Huguenot and the Quaker were combined. Had he lived in times of persecution, he would have resisted unto death any attempt to force upon him the acceptance of a creed, and a submission to doctrines of faith, which the convictions of his conscience would not have allowed him to accept. But his lot having been cast in a free country, and in peaceful times, his life and conversation were illustrative of those evangelical principles of his co-religionists, the Friends, summed up in the language of the inspired Apostle in the words—

"For the grace of God that bringeth salvation hath appeared to all men, teaching us that, denying ungodliness and worldly lusts, we should live soberly, righteously and godly in this present world; looking for that blessed hope, and the glorious appearing of the great God and our Saviour, Jesus Christ; who gave Himself for us, that He might redeem us from all iniquity, and purify unto Himself a peculiar people, zealous of good works."

This personal religion, in-wrought by the Holy Spirit, and influencing the thoughts, words and deeds of Koert Du Bois and Elizabeth, his wife, attracted their neighbors and acquaintances to them, when they had occasion for good counsel and advice. Old and young were in the habit of submitting to them their affairs, and of being guided by their judgment and sound practical common sense. The proprietors of large estates bordering on the Hudson, would seek instruction in regard to the cultivation, preparatory to the beautifying of their lands, from their neighbor and friend, Koert Du Bois. His farm of about six hundred acres he managed with great success. It has never been out of the family, and is now owned in about equal portions by two of his grandsons, Egbert, the son of Peter K., now deceased, and Edward C., the son of Cornelius Du Bois, of Poughkeepsie. Egbert resided upon the homestead, but Edward, formerly the superintendent of the Panama railroad, now resides in Peru, South America, where he married, and is profitably engaged as a civil engineer in the construction of railroads in that country.

Koert Du Bois died 25th April, 1831, aged sixty-eight years and three months. His wife survived him twenty-five years. She died 29th June, 1856, in the eighty-ninth year of her age.

To the foregoing, Egbert D. adds—

In early life he was twice commissioned by the governor as captain of militia, which was then esteemed an honorable post. (This, of course, was before he became a Quaker.) In 1810–'11 he represented Dutchess county in the legislature, but declined a further election. He was a magistrate for many years.

XVI.—Rev. Uriah Du Bois.

BY ROBERT P. DU BOIS.

He was the sixth of the seven children of Peter Du Bois and Amey Greenman. Peter was the eighth of the eleven who sprang from Louis Du Bois and Margaret Jansen. Louis came third among the eleven children who called Jacob Du Bois and Gerritje Gerritsen their father and mother. Jacob was the third of the ten sons and daughters of the original patriarch Louis.

The subject of our notice was born in February, 1768, on the farm of his father, in Pittsgrove township, Salem county, N. J.

There, as a sprightly, good-looking, well-behaved boy, he passed the early part of his life. He was granted the privilege of a classical education; and for that purpose was sent to Orange county, N. Y., for his academical training; and in his twentieth year, he entered the University of Pennsylvania. Here, after three years, in 1790, he graduated. We find him next in Charleston, S. C., engaged in teaching as assistant in an academy, at the same time entering upon theological studies under the Rev. Mr. Keith. At the end of a year he returned to his native State, where he taught awhile in Deerfield and Bordentown; also in the academy at Woodbury, as a tutor of Mr. Hunter, the principal. Here he studied French with a fellow-boarder, and became quite proficient in it.

After a season, he returned to Philadelphia to pursue his preparations for the ministry; this time under the Rev. Ashbel Green, D. D. Here he supported himself mainly by giving lessons in English to a French family. On the 20th of October, 1796, he was licensed to preach by the Presbytery of Philadelphia. As a licentiate, he preached at different places in Pennsylvania, chiefly at Allentown and Deep Run and Tinicum, in Bucks county. His manners were agreeable, his preaching acceptable, and he won the friendship of several of the leading families. He received a joint call from the latter two churches, which he accepted, and was ordained and installed as their pastor on the 16th of December, 1798. The Tinicum congregation was small, but that of Deep Run was of good size for that time. It was founded in 1732; was first styled "Mr. Tennent's Upper Congregation," until 1738, when it took the name of Deep Run.

In the interval between his call and ordination, viz: on the 20th June, 1798, he was married, in Philadelphia, to Martha, daughter of Robert Patterson, LL. D., Professor of Mathematics and Natural Philosophy in the University, in whose family he had boarded whilst a college student, and afterwards when studying theology.

He resided on the parsonage farm at Deep Run until the spring of 1804, when he removed to Doylestown, eight miles to the south, then a growing village, and since 1812 the county seat of Bucks, now a handsome and flourishing borough. He had been invited to become the principal of a large academy just built, and finding the Deep Run congregation declining through the incoming of German families, having also a fondness for teaching, and seeing an opening for the founding of a new church and a suitable place for preaching in the academy, he accepted the invitation. Still retaining his former charges, he now had three places of preaching, besides the care of an academy, the erection of a house for his family and for his boarding students, and the improvement and cultivation of some acres which he had purchased. But being a man of great industry and of untiring activity, he was equal to it all, and carried it on successfully.

The new congregation grew slowly for a while; but in 1813 they felt strong enough to begin a church edifice for themselves. This, with great efforts, chiefly on the part of the pastor and his brother-in-law, Dr. Samuel Moore, was dedicated and occupied in 1815. This, with the recent removal of the county seat to the town, greatly advanced its prosperity, and it has been a growing church ever since. He was earnest in his ministry, and introduced several measures for promoting the cause of his Divine Master which were then considered new. Such were a Sabbath-school, including a school for colored adults, a week-night prayer-meeting, the distribution of tracts, a congregational library, a female prayer-meeting and a Bible class.

As a preacher, he was much esteemed. Several good judges, who were then amongst his hearers, have left written testimonials of his powers and of the impressions for good made upon their minds and the minds of others. His piety was unostentatious. He abhorred sectarian controversy, and loved and co-operated with sincere Christians of every name. At the same time, he was loyal to his own church, and attentive to the meetings of his Presbytery.

During his seventeen years' connection with the academy as the principal of its classical department, he educated large numbers of youths. He threw himself earnestly into this work, and succeeded in imparting knowledge and in training his pupils to think for themselves, as well as in securing their esteem. Many of them afterwards became eminent in church and State, and retained to the last a grateful sense of their obligations to the teacher who had thus given them so happy a start in their life-work.

As a writer, his style was very easy and graceful. He wrote rapidly, and in his lighter productions there was a vein of pleasantry and wit that was very attractive. He wrote his sermons until failing health and eye-sight drove him to extempore preaching, in which he developed unwonted fervor, although he had always distrusted his powers in that direction.

Like all men who lived through the times of our revolution and the forming period of our government, he was, by a kind of necessity, somewhat of a politician. At one time, when the wants of a large and growing family pressed upon him, he held for a few years the civil office of Clerk of the Orphans' Court, in which, however, most of the writing and other business was attended to by his sons, one of whom was then a student of law.

He had a passion for farming, and skill in it, acquired on his father's farm in early life. Under his care, several lots of land, which he had purchased at different times, brought fine crops and abundant fruits.

He was strongly attached to his relatives. Frequently, in his vacations, he paid visits to his old homestead and kindred in New Jersey, though this required at that time a long and tedious journey. With some of them he kept up a correspondence, especially with his blind sister. Most of his children were educated under his own eye and in his own school-room.

No portrait of him was ever taken; but he is remembered as in person of middle size, neat, well-formed, perfectly straight, quick in his movements, active, easy, and expressive in his gestures. His head was round and compact, somewhat bald in later life; his hair a glossy-black; his eyes very dark and sparkling; his nose straight and his chin small. He had a very pleasant smile and a hearty laugh. Though somewhat quick in temper, he was kind and affectionate in his disposition. To this it should be added that he was a man of untiring industry; a good conversationalist; a neat penman, and a good performer upon the flute.

His general health was good, until about two years before his death, the complaint which caused it made its appearance. This was a disease of the kidneys called diabetes, very debilitating, though not painful. Among other effects, it produced a gradual weakening of his vision, until he became at last almost blind. He was put under a diet of strictly animal food, which he conscientiously adhered to, although it called for great self-denial. At this period he presented an interesting object to contemplate. Two congregations, eight miles apart, looked to him as their shepherd; an academy hung upon his hands; a wife and a family of eight children leaned on him for support; and his little farm must not be neglected. Yet, under all this burden, with a weak and emaciated frame, and with almost sightless eyes, he struggled on. Groping his way to the pulpit, and there unable to stand, he preached in a sitting posture; or, shut up in a darkened room, he heard the recitations of classes coming in from the school; and this down almost to the very day of his death. His active spirit knew not how to rest when duty seemed to call.

Although he knew that his end must be near, and expressed himself to brethren who visited him as ready and willing and waiting to go when called, yet he seldom alluded to this in his family. After a Sabbath of increasing weakness, on which he kept his room all the day, he slept well during the night; but early in the morning he raised himself up in the bed, and throwing out his arms, said: "What is this? Is it death?" His wife, seeing the change, replied, "Yes, my dear, it is death!" He lay back upon the pillow, soon became unconscious, and without apparent suffering, after about fourteen hours, he expired without a struggle. This was on the 10th of September, 1821, in the fifty-fourth year of his age, and twenty-third of his ministry.

His funeral was very largely attended; his body was laid near the base of the church he had labored to erect. Two Sabbaths after, his funeral discourse was preached by Dr. Wm. M. Engles, of Philadelphia, his wife's cousin; and the inscription on his tomb ends with the appropriate words: "They that turn many to righteousness, shall shine as the stars for ever and ever."

As the memoir of no married man can be said to be complete without some account of his wife, so it is emphatically in this case. A full account of her ancestry on both sides is contained in the Patterson and Ewing family books. She was born in Cumberland county, N. J., on the 30th of July, 1779, but passed all her single life, except the first year, in the city. She had the best education of the day; was familiar with the French language, and was a skilful performer on the piano, besides being trained to vocal music.

After her husband's death, she kept the family together as far as possible. In 1836 the homestead was sold, and she spent the rest of her days with her two married daughters in Doylestown. Here, peacefully, but not without infirmities, she went down the vale, happy in herself and in her Saviour, helping every good work within her sphere, aiding in the daily cares of the family, corresponding with her absent children and friends, and perusing good books, which she was so well able to appreciate. Upon her mother's decease, at the age of ninety-four years, in 1844, she came into possession of her patrimony, after which her means of support were ample, enabling her to give a much larger scope to her generous and benevolent feelings.

Thus lived our mother through her long life. As her husband's companion, bearing cheerfully the burdens of a pastor's and a boarding-school teacher's wife; as a mother, tender and kind, wise in counsel, safe in her example, self-denying and unselfish almost to a fault; as a Christian, which she was by profession for sixty years, she was faithful to herself and others, exemplifying the attractiveness of "a meek and quiet spirit," entering actively into all her husband's plans for the good of his people, continuing her efforts after his death, acting as librarian of the church library for a long time, and teaching in the Sabbath-school for nearly forty years.

In the leading features of her character, she was retiring, meek, patient, yet active and determined; of a superior, but not showy, intellect; not fluent in conversation, yet not taciturn; an able writer of letters, often spiced with a quiet genuine humor. She was eminently amiable. No one probably can recollect that she was ever angry, or spoke bitterly; yet this was not from apathy or want of decision. It may be truly said that she possessed in a large degree the esteem of the community where she was known throughout the course of life.

Her health was in general good, except that she suffered occasionally, for twenty-five years, from an ailment in her limbs. In December, 1855, she was attacked severely with rheumatism in her limbs. This, with occasional alternations, kept her a prisoner in her room, and often in her bed. In September of the following year the affliction reached her heart—of course, becoming more painful and alarming. In the hours of her pain she was quiet; in the intervals, listening to reading, or examining into her spiritual state. Thus she calmly awaited the change which she knew was coming, and in the full faith of reliance she ceased to breathe, October 25th, 1856.*

XVII.—Charles Ewing Du Bois.

BY REV. R. P. D.

He was the eldest son and child of the Rev. Uriah and Martha P. Du Bois. His birth occurred on the 16th of July, 1799, at the Deep Run parsonage, in Bucks county, Pa. Five years afterwards his parents removed to Doylestown, in the same county, where he continued to reside the rest of his life. He received his education in the Union Academy of that place, under the careful tuition of his father, who was the principal. He studied law under Abraham Chapman, Esq., and was admitted as an attorney on the 28th of August, 1820. In 1823, he was commissioned by the governor as Clerk of the Orphans' Court, and in 1832 he was appointed District Attorney. He also at one time filled the position of Post Master. In 1847, upon the resignation of Mr. Chapman, he was chosen President of the Doylestown Bank, which office he held to the entire satisfaction of all concerned, to his death.

The leading work of his life was as a practising attorney. As a counsellor, in which form of practice he was chiefly employed, his judgment was implicitly confided in by his clients, while his opponents never feared that any unfair advantages would be taken of them. Such trust was placed in his honor and his scrupulous morality, that he was generally known as "the honest lawyer." His opinions were carefully considered before they were given, so that when given they carried weight and commended themselves to the court. His appeals were made to reason and justice and law, rather than to the passions or emotions or prejudices. Through all his life he bore the character of a high-toned, honorable man. In politics, he was never an active partisan, but was always a true lover of his country, and a staunch adherent to the Union. Devoted to his profession, he worthily won an ample competence in its practice.

* They had eight children, all of whom lived to mature age, and all but one were married and had children. Three of the eight are living.

He was married to Mary S., daughter of Rev. John E. Latta, of New Castle, Del. They had a family of eleven children, of whom seven are now living, and two are married. The oldest, John L., who succeeded his father as an attorney-at-law, and his sister Mary, represented their branch in our reunion.

In his early life, Mr. Du Bois was fond of society, but after his marriage he became quite domestic in his habits. His leisure was mainly occupied in improving and adorning his commodious mansion and garden. Besides the care of his own large family, he was of great service to his widowed mother, whom he assisted in managing her affairs and in taking the oversight of his younger brothers and sisters, who will ever remember his valuable efforts in their behalf. He had many warm friends; and as to enemies, he scarcely knew where to find them.

In his younger days he had frequent attacks of bilious fever, but this passed away, and for many years he enjoyed good health. Finally, a complication of diseases befel him, after which he sank rapidly, and, after a season of intense suffering, expired. This was on the morning of March 5th, 1865, in the sixty-sixth year of his age.

XVIII.—Rev. George Du Bois.

Few lives display a more attractive character, or make a better summing-up, than the life of this excellent man, although limited to forty-four years.

He was born at New Paltz, February 27th, 1800, "of Huguenot stock," but the parentage is not stated. We condense the leading details from a discourse by Rev. Dr. Knox, of New York, published in May, 1844.

At the age of fourteen he became a church-member; he then studied for the ministry, and was licensed to preach at *nineteen*. The next year he was pastor of the Reformed church of Bloomingburg, Sullivan county, where he continued three years. He was then called to Franklin Street Church, in New York city, where he labored for fourteen years; when a pulmonary affection began to be developed. He spent a winter in Florida; and on his return took the pastorate at Tarrytown, N. Y., where he finished his course, after a service of seven years. He died April 20th, 1844.

During his ministry in these three churches, about five hundred persons made profession of their faith.—Dr. Knox makes these additional statements—

"His character was one of great consistency and great excellence. He lived and died without reproach. His own example was a living, harmonious, impressive commentary upon the doctrines which are according to godliness, and which he so faithfully proclaimed.

"He possessed a well-endowed, well-furnished and well-balanced mind; and sound discretion, practical wisdom and efficiency of character in an eminent degree.

"His temper was modest, unobtrusive, retiring—at the same time, fearless and resolute when and wherever he believed that he had the call of duty.

"As a preacher, he was evangelical, experimental and practical; grave, solemn and impressive in manner; pointed, pungent and earnest in his appeals; his deep sincerity in the sacred cause was manifest to all.

"In labors, he was abundant and untiring. A diligent student, his preparations for the pulpit were made with the utmost care.

"His last illness was of a character to disqualify him for conversation. His death was peaceful and placid."

XIX.—"Remember the Days of Old."

Gedenkt aen de Dagen van Ouds was the motto of the Ulster Historical Society, fitly stated in Dutch. Our motto, *Gedenkt der vorige Dagen*, is like unto it.

Rev. James Le Fevre, in his address, forcibly remarked: "An old philosopher has said, 'Let us give the past to oblivion; the present to duty; the future to Providence.' This counsel we cannot adopt as to its first member, for that makes the whole impracticable. He who most learns from the past, is most likely to improve the present, and to have a religious hope for the future. Those who rejoice most in the progress and advantages of the present age, realize that all true progress has its roots imbedded in the firm character and strong common-sense of former generations. Those who make an impress for good upon their times are not those who are regardless of their ancestors."

XX.—The Armorial Box.

BY PATTERSON DU BOIS.

Among our family heir-looms, one of the most interesting is the old Silver Box, now in possession of Josiah Du Bois, Esq., of Rondout, N. Y.

Beyond its traditional descent, the engraver's art alone has left upon this treasure its only history; and this we present to our readers to peruse for themselves from the two heliotype fac-similes.

But for the sake of those who are unacquainted with heraldry, we present a brief outline of its symbolic significance and language. And what is here said is given as a matter of historic purport, a "little knowledge" of which need not be in any wise a "dangerous thing" to our democratic ideas.

Although family and national badges have been in vogue from ancient times, yet heraldry, as a fixed and definite science, finds its birth in deeds of knightly valor and royal distinction soon after the Norman conquest, but its greatest impulse arose from the crusades of Richard I. Marks of distinction—national, religious and personal—were recorded in symbolic characters and mottoes upon military "surcoats" and banners. These were matters of pride to those that bore them, and were handed down from generation to generation as the monuments of real or imaginary honor, and the epitome of family history and pedigree.

The principal points in heraldic rules are as follows:—

1. The Shield or Escutcheon is the field or ground on which is represented that which makes up a coat-of-arms; and wherever these figures may be fixed they are represented upon a plane resembling a shield, which may be of any shape desired.

2. Tinctures or Colors of shields and their bearings. These are — *or* (gold), *argent* (silver), *azure* (blue), *gules* (red), *vert* (green), *purpure* (purple), *sable* (black). These colors are represented in engravings by dots and lines.

But where natural objects are presented they may be in their natural colors.

3. Furs are represented by specific marks.

4. Lines, crooked or straight, all having their own titles and significance, divide the field in two, four or more parts, that the arms of several families to which the bearer is allied may be placed in one shield.

5. Charges are divided into three kinds or classes, according to rank and meaning.

(*a.*) *Honorable Ordinaries* are made of lines only, which receive different names according to position and form. They are the Chief, Pale, Bend, Bend-sinister, Fess, Bar, Cheveron, Cross and Saltier.

(*b.*) *Subordinaries* are ancient figures distinguished by specific terms, and are eighteen in number.

(*c.*) *Common Charges* are composed of natural, artificial and chimerical figures.

6. EXTERNAL ORNAMENTS denote the dignity or office of the persons to whom the arms appertain, both amongst the laity and clergy, and consist of Crowns, Coronets, Mitres, Helmets, Mantlings and Supporters. Wreaths, Crests and Scrolls are common to all classes.

Helmets of sovereigns were of burnished gold; princes and lords, of silver figured with gold; knights, steel adorned with silver; private gentlemen, polished steel. They varied in form and position. (That represented in the Du Bois coat-of-arms, given with the paper by Dr. Henry A. Du Bois, is the hemlet of an *esquire* or *gentleman.*)

The *Crest* is the highest part of the ornaments of the coat-of-arms. Crests were formerly marks of great honor, and were only worn by heroes. But this rule has been much modified in modern usage. Crests are as significant of lineage as arms are. They are not assumptive at pleasure; neither can the crest of a maternal ancestor be borne.

The *Scroll* is the ornament placed below the shield, containing a motto or short sentence. This motto may be changed at pleasure, but it often refers to a deed of honor performed by one or all of the family.

Supporters are figures standing on the scroll and aside the escutcheon.

Having thus imperfectly sketched the outlines of heraldic study, we offer what we have said as a key of reference to the engraving on the lid of our Armorial Box.

In the centre is an oval shield, upon which we have distributed the following charges, to wit: A *Cheveron* and *three Pears.* The former of these is an *honorable ordinary*, as already stated; and its form is supposed to symbolize the meeting of the rafters of a house, *i. e.* the uniting of two houses. But this is in dispute. The latter—three pears—is partly natural, and partly chimerical in that the stems are serpent-heads. The intent of this charge is unknown.

As to colors, the box has been so long worn in the pocket, that no lines are left upon the escutcheon; but in the lower corners of the cheveron we find the last traces of the upright lines which originally spread over the entire figure. We see enough to read *gules*—*i. e.* the cheveron was red.

Around the shield we have simply fantastic supporters, which, however, are unimportant, except as a finish. Above it we have the other external ornaments, in the forms of a coronet, two plumes and a unicorn. There is no scroll or motto.

The whole emblazonment, we believe, indicates a lower order of nobility.

It only remains for us to state that, while one side of this box may have meant "nobility" to our ancestors, the simpler blazon of a name and date (1707), on the other side, are our title to the

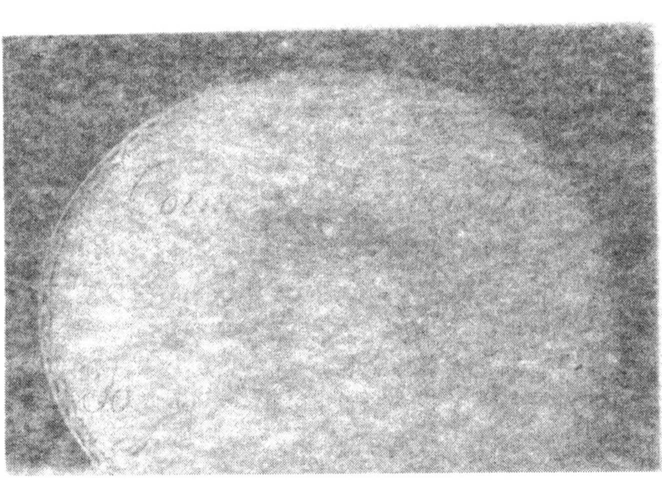

[illegible] the earl [illegible]

[illegible] *Pers.* The [illegible] already stated, and [illegible] of the [illegible] a [illegible]

[illegible] in the pocket, that [illegible] the lower corners of [illegible] upright line which [illegible] We see enough to read [illegible]

[illegible] and we have [illegible] supporters, which [illegible] except as a [illegible] Above [illegible] external ornaments, in the form of a coronet [illegible] and a [illegible] scroll or motto.

[illegible] whole emblazonment, we believe, indicates a lower order [illegible]

[illegible] for us to state that, while one side of this box [illegible] "nobility" [illegible] the [illegible] blazon of a [illegible] date (1[illegible]), on the other side [illegible] to the

Armorial Silver Box. Lower Side.

truer nobility of the soul, which our Huguenot fathers have bequeathed us in the annals of an heroic devotion to their faith. Let us accept the heritage and maintain it by our lives.

It would seem indisputable that this family relic was brought from Europe by Louis Du Bois. Whether our protestantism has cut us off from its further history, which we covet, or whether this hierloom has descended to us through a maternal ancestor, whose lineage we know not, there seems to be no way of ascertaining.

But from the character of those who have carried this box, we cannot entertain a doubt but that it is rightly ours.

Of one fact we are certain,—this relic has been in the family succession for at least *one hundred and seventy years.* As citizens of a republic, we disown the monarchial significance of its blazonry; as Huguenots, we treasure whatsoever our ancestors have left us, and are proud to handle what they have handled and to own what they have owned; but if a few lines of an ancient graver have labelled them gentlemen, let us maintain by *conduct* the meaning of the title.

XXI.—Children's Children.

The editors conclude this compilation by saying, that they have neither the time nor the materials to carry down the various lines of descent from Louis. Probably no individual or partnership could or would undertake it. Nor would it be desirable. Most of such details would be of limited interest, and it would make an unwieldy and costly book. We therefore follow out a good suggestion, and add blank leaves, where each family can, with pen and ink, keep up its own record more appropriately than in a family Bible.*

* We do not counsel the same liberality of expense and trouble, but we will state that, in 1865, a grandson of Thomas Du Bois, of Pittsgrove, N. J., printed a small edition pertaining to his own branch; and not only that, but reprinted and prefixed the Du Bois Record, which was already out of print, and not to be had. The author (Thomas) and his father and son, were at the reunion.

XXII.—Louis, a Magistrate.

At the last minute of the twelfth hour (of this book), Anson Du Bois finds the following bit of colonial history, which he and we think worthy of insertion, even if it comes out of place:—

"Lowies du Bois, Magistrate of the Town of Horly, complaining by petition that Roelof Swartwout is gone to dwell on the Flatland contrary to order; and that two Frenchmen, residing in the Town of Horly, refuse to take the oath of allegiance—

"It is ordered, In the case of Swartwout, petitioner is referred to the Court of deputed Councillors in the Esopus. As regards the Frenchmen, the schout [an executive officer] shall order them instantly to depart, unless they take the oath of allegiance to the Government; and to remain quiet in case of any attack by their nation."—(*Brodhead's Doc. History of N. Y.*)

This petition was addressed to the governor, in 1674. It settles the fact not only of Louis' residence in Hurley, but of his being the head man there. Although we have given him so many honors already, it is but fair we should add this also.

Dr. Du Bois states that this Swartwout was the first sheriff under the charter given to Wiltwyck (Kingston) by Governor Stuyvesant, in 1661. The Flatland, where he had unlawfully settled, was a tract of meadow or pasture land common to the people of the town, such as they had also at Kingston.

XXIII.—Finale from France.

Eugene Du Bois sends the following from his correspondent, M. C. Du Bois-Gregoire, U. S. Consul, dated February 15th, 1876:— "An old man, descended from the Du Bois family at Wicres, and of the same name, came to speak to me several times at Lille. He was eighty years old, and affirmed, according to the tradition from his fathers, that there never was any other than the one family at Wicres, and that this ascends to *Chretien* Du Bois as its head." This also is our *pater familias*.

NAMES OF SUBSCRIBERS.

James G. Du Bois,	New York city,	15 copies.
John W. D.,	New Paltz, N. Y.	
Jacob G. D.,	do.	2 copies.
George D.,	do.	
Deyo D.,	do.	
Henry M. D.,	do.	
Peter W. D.,	do.	
Chester D.,	Utica, N. Y.	
George D.,	do.	
Elnora D.,	Ohioville, N. Y.	
Elizabeth D.,	Poughkeepsie, N. Y.	
Rev. Hasbrouck D.,	New York city.	
William M. D.,	Elmira, N. Y.,	10 copies.
William L. D.,	Catskill, N. Y.,	10 copies.
John D.,	Wappenger's Falls, N. Y.,	5 copies.
Dr. John Coert D.,	Hudson, N. Y.,	20 copies.
Barent S. D.,	Catskill, N. Y.	
T. Vandeveer D.,	Freehold, N. J.,	3 copies.
Gilbert D.,	Napanoch, N. Y.,	10 copies.
Elijah D.,	Kingston, N. Y.,	5 copies.
John L. D.,	Doylestown, Pa.,	4 copies.
John D.,	Freehold, N. J.	
Livingston D.,	do.	
Egbert D.,	Salt Point, Dutchess, N.Y.,	6 copies.
Preston D.,	Moorston, N. Y.	
A. McKim D.,	Carlinsville, Ill.,	10 copies.
Charles D.,	Fishkill, N. Y.	
Rev. Anson D.,	Flatlands, Long Island,	15 copies.
Dr. H. H. D.,	Bridgewater, Conn.,	3 copies.
Dr. Henry A. D.,	New Haven, Conn.,	15 copies.
Cornelius D.,	Staten Island, N. Y.,	20 copies.
Robert D.,	Bridgeton, N. J.,	3 copies.

Rev. Robert P. D.,	New London, Pa.,	5 copies.
Dr. Frank L. D.,	U. S. Navy,	5 copies.
Rev. George W. D.,	Faribault, Minn.,	5 copies.
Dr. T. W. D.,	Poughkeepsie, N. Y.,	2 copies.
Josiah D.,	Rondout, N. Y.	
Edward D.,	Marlborough, N. Y.	
J. Dill D.,	Portland, Oregon,	5 copies.
J. W. D.,	Lapier, Michigan,	2 copies.
Benjamin D.,	Freehold, N. J.	
H. A. D.,	Philadelphia,	5 copies.
William E. D.,	do.	10 copies.
William L. D.,	do.	15 copies.
Patterson D.,	do.	5 copies.
Luther D.,	Kingston, N. Y.,	2 copies.
S. S. D.,	Oxford, Indiana.	
Rev. B. D. Wyckoff,	Olyphant, Luzerne, Pa.,	2 copies.
Dr. P. D. Hornbeek,	Wawarsing, N. Y.	
Asa Le Fever,	New Paltz, N. Y.,	2 copies.
Rev. J. K. Rhinehart,	Princetown, Albany county, N. Y.	
A. S. Schoonmaker,	Gardiner, N. Y.	
A. V. N. Eltinge,	New Paltz, N. Y.	
Ira Deyo,	do.	
A. P. Le Fever,	do.	
Rev. James Le Fever,	Middlebush, Somerset county, N. J.	
Mrs. Alfred Wagstaff,	Long Island, N. Y.,	20 copies.
Mrs. Mary E. Gould,	New Haven,	3 copies.
Prof. W. H. Brewer,	Yale College,	5 copies.
W. Du Bois Miller,	Fidelity Trust, Phila.,	2 copies.
J. B. Eckfeldt,	U. S. Mint, Phila.	
Isaac P. Schenck,	Franklin, Ohio.	
Mrs. B. I. Relyea,	Westport, Conn.,	2 copies.
Peter Crispell, Jr.,	Hurley, N. Y.	
Dr. G. D. Crispell,	Kingston, N. Y.	
Miss Laura F. Cooper,	Nanuet, Rockland, N. Y.	
Peter J. Du Bois,	Kingston, N. Y.,	5 copies.
C. G. Fowler,	Newburgh, N. Y.,	2 copies.
Isaac Du Bois,	Ohioville, N. Y.	
Josiah Hasbrouck,	New Paltz, N. Y.,	2 copies.

Theodore Deyo,	New Paltz, N. Y.	
Rev. E. T. Corwin,	Somerset County, N. J.	
Rev. Philip Peltz,	New Paltz.	
Cornelius Du Bois,	Poughkeepsie,	4 copies.
Mrs. C. M. Stewart,	Philadelphia,	2 copies.
Mrs. Rebecca J. Parmele,	Willow Creek, Tompkins co., N. Y.	
Miss Emma Parmele,	do. do.	
Maj. Gen. W. S. Hancock,	U. S. Army.	
Oliver D. Russell,	New York.	
Mrs. J. W. Schermerhorn,	do.	
A. D. Du Bois,	do.	
James D.,	Int. Rev. Office, Washington.	
S. L. D.,	Rosendale, Ulster, N. Y.	
Miss Elsie Le Fever,	New Paltz,	2 copies.
Henry D.,	do.	2 copies.
Granville R. Person,	Catskill, N. Y.	
John A. Cooke,	do.	
Andrew E. Elmore,	Madison, Wis.,	2 copies.
A. H. Vandling,	Scranton, Penna.	
E. H. Thomas,	Portland, Maine.	

INDEX.

PROCEEDINGS.

NOTES AND ADDITIONS.

ILLUSTRATIONS.

THE END.

Milton Keynes UK
Ingram Content Group UK Ltd.
UKHW022249080124
435706UK00005B/317